MALAYAN SCOUTS SAS

MALAYAN SCOUTS SAS

A MEMOIR OF THE MALAYAN EMERGENCY, 1951

J.C. DURKIN

SPELLMOUNT

This book is dedicated to my father, Joe Durkin Sr, who did not live to see his words
in print, and to my mother, Dorothy.

I also include my father's own dedication: 'To ten men, now also dead.'

'Dead faces laugh. King! King! Dead faces laugh.'
The King's Threshold, W.B. Yeats.

First published in 2011
by Spellmount, an imprint of The History Press
The Mill, Brimscombe Port
Stroud, Gloucestershire, GL5 2QG
www.thehistorypress.co.uk

© J. C. Durkin, 2011

The right of J. C. Durkin to be identified as the Author
of this work has been asserted in accordance with the
Copyrights, Designs and Patents Act 1988.

British Library Cataloguing in Publication Data.
A catalogue record for this book is available from the British Library.

ISBN 978 0 7524 6110 6

Typesetting and origination by The History Press
Printed in Great Britain

CONTENTS

INTRODUCTION TO THE AUTHOR

My father, Joseph Christopher Durkin, was born in the small market town of Athy in the County of Kildare in December 1929. His father Patrick Murray-Durkin had been born in New York City but for reasons unknown went back to live in Ireland, where he met and married his wife Mary Scully. Ireland was then at peace if not with itself then at least with England, but the country was poor, poor enough for his family to make the move to Liverpool just before the outbreak of the Second World War. Patrick would tell me later that England was the last place he wanted to go to, the family 'were never happy, we should have gone to the States'. Liverpool was a city divided along sectarian lines, much like Belfast or Glasgow. The family found accommodation in the Scotland Road area, a huge slum to the north of the city centre running down towards the docks. My father would always remember the district as 'that sectarian ghetto by the sea'. It was an unpleasant place for Irish Catholics to be and the family soon moved to Southport, a large town to the north of Liverpool.

When the war started my grandfather Patrick rejoined the army – he had served with the Leinster Regiment during the First World War. He was discharged from the army in 1945 with the substantive rank of Corporal and awarded a pension and the War Medal 1939-45, an award his son would also gain. Patrick had served with the British Army in two world wars, but also with the losing side in the Irish Civil War and had been interned for some time in Mountjoy Gaol, Dublin by the Free State government, only his American citizenship saving him from longer incarceration. It might seem strange for Irish 'Republicans' to be serving with the British Army but it has always been the norm in Ireland itself. This strand of Republicanism would later cause much suffering to my father and his family.

My father was a teenager in 1945 and held a buff (juvenile) identity card, which prevented him from joining up, something he was keen to do. The war in Europe had ended but the one against Japan continued and he was determined to play a part in it. His father's blue identity card was the answer to his problem and he duly presented himself at the local Labour Exchange with the card to register for service. A month later on 2 August 1945 he was called up to serve for 'the duration of emergencies'. He was fifteen years and seven months old.

The war in the east came to an end just after completion of his initial training with 61 Primary Training Wing and that seemed to be that; he had gone to a lot of trouble to little purpose. There was a small consolation in that his service, though short, gave him entitlement to the War Medal 1939-45 and as far as I know he was one of the youngest holders of this award. He was transferred to the Army Air Corps and posted to No 1 Parachute Regiment Infantry Training Centre, where he stayed from September 1945 to January 1946. He was always interested in aviation and liked to tell me that his training with the Air Corps had taught him to fly basic aircraft, which he said was a very simple task 'that pilots like to make look difficult with all those instruments that were never used for anything.' I gave him the benefit of the doubt on this. I would ask him about whether he was ever frightened of 'jumping'; his response was that when enplaned with a 'stick' of say twelve men 'it would be a brave man who refused to jump', but he admitted that he was frightened on his first few jumps from a tethered balloon at Ringway Airport, Manchester.

Hearing that reinforcements were being put together for the King's Regiment, then serving against the communist army in Greece, he volunteered for this campaign, but in the meantime the authorities had discovered his true age and in May 1946 he was discharged from the army having been found to have fraudulently enlisted. The rider to this stated that his service and medal entitlement were not affected in any way and the service would count towards a pension when re-enlisting. On leaving the army he joined the Merchant Navy as a deck hand and saw a bit of the world.

In March 1948, three months after his eighteenth birthday he was recalled to the army to carry out National Service and served with the 1st Lancashire Fusiliers until

May 1951, having signed on for a further three years. While with the regiment he was cruiser weight champion of the battalion in 1948, 1949 and 1950 and was awarded boxing colours in 1950. Early in 1951 – the regiment was then serving in Egypt – a notice appeared on the company notice board calling for volunteers to serve in the Far East with the Malayan Scouts SAS and he put his name forward. Some months later on 1 June he was on his way to Malaya to serve in D Squadron. The Scouts did the work required of them and without interference from army 'brass'. It is significant that during the short life of the regiment the insurgents pulled their horns in and for the first time in the campaign lost the initiative.

Towards the end of 1951 and seemingly without reason the regiment was posted to barracks in Singapore. This caused a lot of unrest, the men seeing it as a slap in the face. He remained in Malaya but kept in touch with events by regular visits to Selerang barracks. He returned there in December and on the 23rd was 'badged' – the practice of formally presenting troopers with the beret and wings badge of the SAS – by Major John Woodhouse, the 'Old Fox'. My father had huge affection and respect for Woodhouse whom he considered to be an excellent soldier who was 'very fair minded and tough as they come', not an epithet easily given within the SAS. Major Woodhouse would go on later to become the Commanding Officer of 22 SAS Regiment.

On 1 January 1952, convinced that the regiment was out of the campaign for good, he asked for a transfer to an infantry regiment still engaged up-country. This

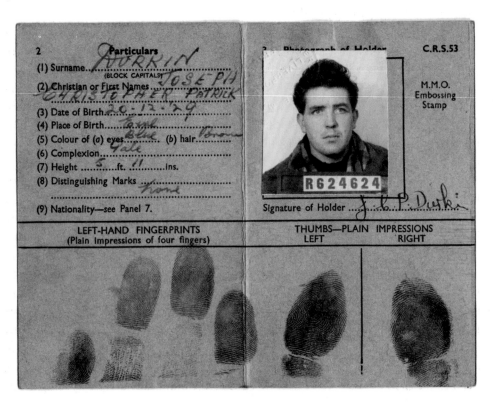

Trooper Joseph Durkin.

was not granted and soon afterwards he took part in Operation *Titus* with elements of A and D Squadrons. However, he was still not happy with the way that the war was being fought and asked for and was granted a transfer to the Manchester Regiment. Although formally no longer a member of the SAS he would always stress that 'you never ever left, it was not possible, you just knew too much', and claimed that he continued to carry out 'jobs' for them. I never enquired what these might be and to be frank, I was frightened and felt it best not to know.

He served in Malaya for a further year, 132 days more than the period he had re-enlisted for. He was discharged and transferred to the reserve in April 1953 and on completion of reserve he was asked to re-enlist for a further three years. This he did, finally being discharged on 28 February 1964.

After his service with the army he came home, but not having any obvious workplace skills he enrolled at a government training centre in Liverpool to learn basic construction skills. It was a six-month programme and my father enjoyed it and learnt a great deal. On completion and with some money he had received on leaving the army he set up in business as a building contractor and was rather successful. I put this down to his politeness and respect for the customer, and his way of always keeping to time and budget, things he had learned in the army. If I ever mentioned his politeness his response was that 'in the SAS to be rude was a fool's game and not lightly undertaken.'

At this time in the mid-fifties he met and married my mother Dorothy Houghton; she would be the one constant for the rest of his life sharing the troubles he would bring on himself and her, always supportive, loving and kind. He developed an interest in books and antiques, and it became something of a passion and took over from the construction work altogether in time. He loved buying and selling, going to auctions, discovering a rare first edition or buying something for a price he knew he could sell on at a profit. There was also his writing, every night at the kitchen table, pencil in hand making notes about magpies, greyhounds and ferrets, turning them

The author and his family after leaving the British Army.

into stories. He also wrote a book about collecting antiques and articles for *Lancashire Life*.

In 1969 violence erupted in Northern Ireland over the oppression of the minority Catholic population and eventually the British Army had to step in. This spurred my father into action, writing to MPs, sending letters to newspapers and organising meetings. He also wrote to leading Republican leaders offering his services and to other ex-soldiers, asking them to act as a buffer force between the Catholics and the police force. He called for Ireland to be united through force of arms.

He then took the fateful step of writing to officers of the Royal Green Jackets Regiment calling for them to desert along with their men. He was arrested and charged under the Incitement to Disaffection Act and imprisoned awaiting trial. He was found guilty at Liverpool Crown Court but was not given a custodial sentence. His so-called co-conspirator Michael Tobin was not so lucky and received the maximum sentence of two years from another court. He did 'hard time' in Chelmsford prison where PIRA sympathisers were not particularly liked.

Life was never the same after the trial; after all, it is one thing to be a republican sympathiser in Belfast, Derry or Dublin but to be one in Southport, Lancashire is quite another. My father carried on campaigning but this time on environmental issues (before they became fashionable, he was ahead of his times in some things) and animal rights. I never really thought his heart was in it but I suppose he had to do something, and he continued with his books and antiques.

It was only late in his life that my father would talk about his army experiences, mainly I think due to the effect they had on him, which is to say not good. However, in order to write this book he had to discuss his life with the army in order to structure the work and get the ideas into the open. He always used to write in longhand, usually with a pencil at the kitchen table, late at night, and I would sit opposite him, a sounding board. Initially I could hardly believe some of the situations he would recount, the

The author in his later years (left) at an SAS reunion.

secret prisons, the arrests, the torturing of prisoners and always the killings. It is only now, given what we know about the war in Iraq and all the other 'wars on terror', that I believe him. He would only write down what he considered to be suitable and believable, the rest we just discussed, and maybe that is for the best. He was always good with animals and writing about them, which is why he included the passages on the SAS mules and the camp monkeys. He thought people would like the stories and if you read the manuscript it is mostly upbeat and positive; this is what he wanted to provide to his wider audience, not the violence.

My mother Dorothy died suddenly in December 1999. It was a shock to us all and propelled my father into an eventual nervous collapse fuelled by alcohol. It was only because he was so physically strong and mentally tough that he survived as long as he did. He told me he would like to commit suicide but as that was a mortal sin he could not bring himself to do it. He asked me on more than one occasion if I would shoot him to put him out of misery: 'Quick and clean Joseph, I will tell you how to go about it.' I obviously refused but it was frightening and very disturbing because he meant what he said. When he got to a condition where the family could no longer give him care at home he was taken to the local hospital. In one of the last conversations I had with him before he died I asked what troubled him so; he replied it was the 'force of evil' that sat on his shoulder and taunted him about the wrongs he had carried out. I said this was nonsense but he would not have it; he took the guilt with him to the very end and I felt it drove him mad.

He died on 5 May 2001, twenty years after another spirited Irishman, Bobby Sands, died in the Maze prison. I am sure my Dad would have appreciated that.

Joseph Durkin (Jr)
Manchester

ACKNOWLEDGEMENTS

I would like to thank several people for their help with bringing my father's work to the wider world. Daniel Bowerbank and Leanne Hall for IT support, and the following for the images used in the book: John Robertson, Julian Bond, Phillip Kier, Peter Lammin, Ian Thomas and John, Doug, Chris, Paul and Andrew Chatfield. I would also like to say a big thank you to my editor Miranda Jewess for having faith in this project. As ever though, for her patience and support, my thanks go out to my wife Caroline and daughter Katie.

PROLOGUE

On the evening of 14 December 1941, six men entered the Italian airfield near the coastal town of Tamet in North Africa, moving quietly in the dark to evade the sentries. On coming upon a group of buildings, one of the men, a large bearded figure, stopped and listened carefully before going inside one of them. He did so confidently, as if going through his own front door. The occupants, enjoying a social evening, did not notice him immediately and he shot those nearest to him before they had time to move. Others jumped to their feet and he shot them too, then dispatched others who were still frozen in their places. When the magazine of the sub-machine gun he had used to such deadly effect was empty he put it aside and calmly unholstered a .38 revolver. He picked off the remainder with carefully aimed shots. When they were all down he holstered the revolver, picked up the sub-machine gun and left the building. Inside it all the pilots of the planes on the airfield were either dead or dying.

On the perimeter of the field the sentries, now alert, swivelled machine guns inwards directing a hail of fire at the raiders. They went to ground quickly, crawling under and out of the arcs of fire, escaping unharmed into the desert. There they rested, listening to the ongoing fire behind them. When it stopped the leader of the group spoke. It was now time to carry out the mission proper, the destruction of the planes on the airfield.

Prior to the earlier work of the evening most of the group, seasoned soldiers, would have argued about the wisdom of this but now saved their breath. They had been told that Lieutenant Paddy Mayne was not a man to argue with and his actions further reinforced this. He had decided and that was that.

It was pitch dark when they retraced their steps, again getting onto the airfield without opposition. Once there they went about their work methodically fixing delayed action explosives to every plane, doing the same at ammunition and fuel dumps. When every available target had been attended to they withdrew to listen to the sound of explosions rending the cold night air. Twenty-four aircraft were put out of action in the raid and all ammunition and fuel dumps were destroyed. The six-man raiding party returned to base without loss. L Detachment of the Special Air Service 'Brigade' had completed its first successful operation against the Axis Forces in the Second World War.

1

THE BIRTH OF A REGIMENT

At the time of the successful and bloody raid on Tamet, L Detachment had been in existence for little more than four months, a period dogged by failure and with a growing awareness that its survival was problematic. The raid changed that, proving that a guerrilla force with the right leadership could wreak havoc in the enemy rear, out of all proportion to the number of men employed. That had been the object of the force from its inception. The success also caused some to think that a new chapter on the art of war had been written, but this was not the case. The raid was no more than a variation on a theme – infiltration. The Germans had used the tactic through-out the First World War, attacking, not in waves as the British and French did but in small groups over a wide front, filtering through defence systems, suffering mini-mum casualties and causing maximum disruption. During the Second World War they again used the tactic, deploying airborne troops instead of the more usual foot soldiers. Their success during the Battle of France was impressive, convincing many, including General Bernard Law Montgomery – who sometimes failed to spot the obvious – that a new era had indeed dawned. Paras were the way ahead and the British Army was incomplete without them. The War Office agreed, but failed to differentiate between the tactic and the means of its implementation. It was an error that would prove costly to the British at Arnhem, although also to the Germans during the invasion of Crete. But that lay in the future. In the meantime recruitment for the new force began and by October 1940 there was a cadre of 300 with as many more in training. The rush of recruits had more than a little to do with the fact that qualified parachutists – those who had completed at least eight jumps – were paid two shillings a day over and above the three shillings paid to ordinary infantrymen. In December 1940 the cadre took part in a corps exercise on Salisbury Plain; Montgomery designated it grandly as the Special Air Service Brigade. Its role in the exercise was to demonstrate the value – or otherwise – of airborne troops in desert warfare. When the exercise ended the consensus was that a value existed – speed in deployment – but little more than this.

In spite of the lukewarm reception the brigade was retained, going on to become the Parachute Regiment.

The birth of the SAS proper came about through a mixture of intent, good timing and pure chance. In the summer of 1941 a junior officer serving in the Eighth Army, Lieutenant David Stirling, put a proposal to the Commander in Chief General Claude 'The Auk' Auchinleck setting out his idea for the creation of an airborne force with a difference. Unlike Montgomery's Brigade (or General Kurt Student's blitzkrieg paras), it would operate in small groups — another variation, if minor, on a familiar theme — parachuting onto selected target areas under the cover of darkness. There it would act in a guerrilla role, disrupting supply lines, destroying aircraft on the ground and generally keeping the Germans and Italians on the back foot.

The idea appealed to Auchinleck. He had only been in command of Eighth Army for a month and from the very beginning Prime Minister Winston Churchill had been nagging him to do something, anything, to show that the army was doing what it was

Lieutenant David Stirling (far right) in the desert as part of L Detachment during the first months of the SAS.

supposed to do. As the trickle of 'action at all costs' messages from Downing Street was threatening to become a flood, Stirling appeared as if on cue. The Auk was delighted. Here it seemed was a way out of his predicament – and at little cost. The proposed raiding force, though unlikely to make any spectacular returns, might just be capable of setting off enough fireworks to convince Churchill that something was being done. Eighth Army was not ready for offensive action and anything that could save it from committal to battle before it was had to be worth a try. Permission to raise the force was granted and as an acknowledgement of Montgomery's prior if peripheral role in the matter, it was designated L Detachment of his by now phantom SAS Brigade.

Stirling recruited for the Detachment amongst the various commando units then inactive in the Egyptian Canal Zone and found the going hard. The commandos had heard it all before and were not impressed by the would-be recruiting sergeant – or the prospect of landing in the middle of the Afrika Korps while still attached to the harness of a parachute. But in spite of the poor response Stirling persisted and eventually managed to persuade 68 men of all ranks. The infant force that would become the SAS Regiment was born, and apart from a few false starts it would go on to achieve great success. This success would come in part because of the recruitment of one particular officer, Lieutenant Blair Mayne.

Mayne was an Irishman born in north-east Ulster with a leaning towards nationalism, making this known at every opportunity. His adoption of the name 'Paddy' – the only one he would answer to outside a close circle of family and friends – was a deliberate act, challenging those in the habit of using it in a derogatory sense. It was his particular way of trailing the coat, daring anyone to step on it. Some did, testing their belief in racial superiority, and were soon converted. His reputation as a fighting man both on and off the battlefield was without parallel; he was the personification of Strabo's Celt, 'madly fond of war, high spirited and quick to do battle'. His leadership and prowess in war ensured the survival of the fledgling SAS and earned it a place in the folklore of the common soldier.

Training began at the end of August and was completed early in November and L Detachment was now ready for operational duty. On the evening of 16 November 1941 the unit emplaned for raids on the airfields at Tamimi and Gazala, preludes to the 'Crusader' offensive to be launched by Auchinleck two days later. The start line for the offensive was well within striking range of planes from both airfields, and troops massing for the assault would present ideal targets. The task of the SAS was to prevent that happening, destroying the Axis planes before the build up of troops on the start line began on the following evening – 17 November. It was an onerous task.

Strangely, in view of Stirling's original concept of a small force, all bar four of his command were committed to the raids. He was tempting fate, as 20 men – 10 to each airfield – would have been sufficient for the stealthy work. In committing more he was being over anxious, reasoning that if 20 men could do the job, 64 could do it that much better. The operation was ill-starred from the beginning. Prior to emplaning, weather reports had made it clear that conditions for the following 12 hours would be

The men of L
Detachment
SAS group.

unsuitable for airborne operations. Gale force winds were forecast for the operational area and would be at their height when the planes arrived over the DZ. Stirling was aware of this but felt compelled to go on; the new force had to prove itself, it was imperative. He had promised results and had to deliver. The result was disastrous.

Almost as soon as the planes were airborne they flew into the centre of an electrical storm, fuelled by a mass of cloud that covered every mile of the flight path. High winds blew, throwing the transports around like leaves. On arrival over the DZ the storm continued to rage but in spite of the deadly conditions the jump went ahead. The action proved the courage of the men but perhaps a lack of judgement and too much faith in their superiors, as the majority jumped out into eternity. Even the pugnacious Mayne made the jump, swiftly followed by the ten other men in his plane. In the end only 22 members of L Detachment survived to return safely to their own lines. Not one shot was fired in anger throughout the operation, the casualties all arising from the failure to reconsider what had become a changed situation, given the weather. The first SAS operation could easily have been its last.

Stirling gained a valuable lesson from the debacle and relearned another: flying to and parachuting onto a target area is not necessarily the best way of getting men from A to B and bigger is not always better. In future operations the SAS would travel to their targets in customised jeeps and return to first principles, confining raiding parties to no more than ten men. This would remain the case – with one further disastrous exception – until the war moved to Europe.

The pattern was set by Mayne when with five men he had carried out the first attack on Tamet aerodrome. He repeated the exercise two weeks later when with four ORs he revisited the airfield where a fresh batch of planes awaited their attention. There was spirited opposition to the second visit but in spite of it the previous tally was beaten, 27 planes being put out of action. In a period of 14 days, with an under-strength section, he had accounted for 51 enemy aircraft – The Auk was getting jackpot returns from his small investment.

Many raids similar to those at Tamet were carried out in the New Year, most of them highly successful. Those few that were not taught valuable lessons, put to good use in future operations. On some of the raids it was necessary to don mufti for security reasons, the raiders dressing as Arabs, and on at least one occasion the men travelled to the target area in the company of their enemies. The practice breached the Geneva Convention on the conduct of war and aroused a lot of controversy, largely ignored by the British High Command but acted on by Hitler. He issued an order which in effect was a death warrant for any commando or other enemy personnel captured behind the German lines – in or out of uniform. In future they were to be put to death on the spot. The order, itself also in breach of the Geneva Convention, gave a quasi-legality to those who disguised themselves in order to escape capture. It would have been foolish to do otherwise. The order was ignored during the North African campaign on the instructions of Field Marshal Erwin Rommel, which, in one notable instance, was fortunate for the SAS.

As raid succeeded raid the fame of L Detachment spread, but in spite of this volunteers were not coming forward in the numbers expected. There was a steady trickle, sufficient to keep the raiding parties up to strength but not enough to make the Detachment something grander. The fact that it was an elite force had its drawbacks; it could not be allotted reinforcements by a stroke of the C in C's pen. Rather, would-be members had first to select themselves and then be reselected by either Mayne or Stirling, who spent little time on such things during the early months of 1942, and the unit remained an ephemeral thing surviving from day to day. It was part of the army but on the fringe, unable to attain the cachet of regimental status. This was a matter of concern to Stirling but he could see no way of altering the situation. In the end numbers were boosted by an event in Algeria – then controlled by Vichy France – an event that would lead to L Detachment swelling to many times its original 120 members, sufficient for a regiment, and just as importantly would introduce a Gallic elan to the Detachment which would be the means of increasing the flow of volunteers from Eighth Army.

In January 1942 the many Germans serving in the French Foreign Legion in Algeria had decided that the time had come for them to move on. The war was passing them by and they wanted to fight for their Fatherland. The Vichy authorities, ever eager to serve German interests, met with their representatives and readily agreed not only to their going but to their request that they leave as a disciplined body, a regiment. At the end of the month 1,000 German legionnaires marched away from the French Army of Africa and joined Rommel's Afrika Korps in the western desert. A month later, after a probationary period as a labour battalion, Rommel designated it the 361st Infantry Regiment and gave it a place in the order of battle.

During the following seven months the Regiment distinguished itself in the fighting leading up to the second and last battle of El Alamein. In that pounding match it was destroyed but the example set by the men who had formed it lived on. Their action had infuriated many of their fellow legionnaires who had watched them go, particularly the Alsatians – Frenchmen classified as foreigners when the Legion was in need of recruits, and as French when Germany laid claim to Alsace-Lorraine, their homeland – the most numerous national group in the Legion after their departure, and men with no love for Germany. They talked, arguing that as one group had been allowed to go they should be allowed to do the same. They put their case to the Legion Commandant but without success. Theirs was a different case as their object was to join the British, not the Germans. If they insisted on going it would have to be by the back door and the Legion band would not play them off. They had to desert and did so in droves and in mortal danger, death a certainty if caught.

Escape from the Legion was not easy but escape from Algeria to Egypt was so difficult as to be almost impossible. Seas of sand and the Axis armies barred the way by land and the waters were guarded by German patrol boats. Some Alsatians travelled by the scenic route, going westwards instead of eastwards arriving in Egypt via Morocco and Gibraltar. Others took the more direct and dangerous route, many of them dying in transit. *Goumiers* – mounted Arab auxiliaries of the Legion – hunted them down without respite. The auxiliaries had been recruited specially for the purpose of catching deserters, and while they were not under orders to kill they were not forbidden to do so, their instructions ambivalent – 'capture or kill'. It seemed that a choice existed but it did not. Payment was by results, the same bounty for a dead man as a live one, the same for a severed head as for the whole body. As heads were easier to manage – a dozen heads was easier to transport than one live prisoner – market forces were against the survival of any deserter taken by them. A deserter – whether alive or just a disembodied head – commanded the price of 25 francs. It was a lot of money, if only in a comparative sense. In 1942 a legionnaire was paid 2 francs 4 centimes a day, equal to 10 US cents or 5 English pence. The Goumier, if attentive to his work, could earn ten times that amount in a few productive hours and many became relatively rich men between February and December 1942.

The sea route to Egypt, while it meant escaping the attentions of the Goumiers, put the Alsation legionaries in the crosshairs of the Germans. They controlled the coastal waters from Oran to Alexandria, making the route almost as hazardous as the overland one. While death at their hands was not always an immediate prospect for deserters, it was certain when handed over to the French. Paradoxically, the Legion while not overly concerned about the activities of the Goumiers did not have a policy of executing either captured deserters – the few taken either by the civil or military police – or those returning to service of their own free will. This changed when the Germans – concerned about the spate of desertions to the British and Free French forces – ordered the Vichy authorities to set up a special military court to deal with the matter, and made the death sentence mandatory for all found guilty. The change brought about by the policy destroyed what had been an important part of the ethos of the Legion.

Prior to 1942, desertion was seen as part and parcel of the learning process that went into the making of a legionnaire. It was an act that all attempted, demonstrating initiative and courage, a game played to set rules, death at the hands of the auxiliaries if lost, acceptance by all if won. Winning had nothing to do with making a permanent break from service but everything to do with outfacing the dangers involved in the attempt. The whole purpose of the exercise was to remain free for the period required to establish the commission of the offence in military law – five days – as opposed to the 21 days applying in the British Army. During this time the civil and military police had to be evaded as well as an army of touts; 25 francs was as great a sum to them as it was to the Goumiers. The game was lost if falling into the hands of the police, lost without hope of a replay if taken by the auxiliaries, won when the deserter, after the elapse of the statuary period returned to barracks of his own volition. He was then a legionnaire, a valuable asset to the regiment and the State – but still liable for punish–ment. This did not involve due process and if borne stoically enhanced reputation. It was decided on and administered by a Sous-Chef with discretion, a savage beating or the award of up to an hour *en crapaudine*, trussed like an oven ready chicken. It was an exemplary punishment, causing pain without dulling the senses as a kick or a blow from the fist would, the recipient aware of it from the first to the last moment. It was a punishment that would only be awarded if the Sous-Chef was in a particularly bloody minded, vindictive mood and even then he would rarely allow it to go on for more than 30 minutes, an hour often too long causing crippling injuries and the loss of a soldier to France.

When awarded the punishment was carried out immediately, the prisoner tied in the approved manner, leaving six feet of rope hanging, the wheel of a thumbscrew loosing or tightening the bonds as required, allowing circulation or stopping it, causing unimaginable pain. When freed from the rope the limbs were unable to function and the shriven offender was carried to the barrack room with leave to rest for 24 hours. During this time the pain could be borne in the knowledge that he was now accepted as an equal by his companions and as a soldier of worth by officers and NCOs. En Crapaudine was a savage punishment with the compensation that it was over and done with quickly, infinitely preferable to service in a penal battalion, the alternative if a man refused to accept summary punishment.

When the Germans forced a change in the rules, desertion from the Legion became more than a deadly game with an even chance of winning or losing. The military court set up at the behest of the Germans to try deserters was in constant session throughout 1942 and the early days of 1943. Every legionnaire appearing before it, invariably Alsatian, was condemned to death, the Court assuming – without evidence to the fact – that the deserter's intentions had been to join the British and that he was therefore guilty of treason as well as desertion. That being the case they were denied the last privilege of a soldier, death by firing squad, and were instead handed over to the public executioner and guillotined as common criminals. Those legionnaires who did make it to Egypt came together with like-minded men who had left Legion

David Stirling in the Western Desert. He wears the SAS officer's cap.

An early photograph of 'Paddy' Blair Mayne.

regiments in Syria with the same purpose in mind. The two groups, after discussions on the best way forward, opted for the SAS. It was an obvious choice; they were paras as well as legionnaires.

In the preceding nine months Stirling's raiders had been applying fire and sword to the Axis forces. Now with the French and Alsatians effectively transforming L Detachment into a regiment the opportunities were endless, the attacks could be extended, applied in a hundred places and all at one and the same time.

But it was not to be, as the Regiment was now given an infantry role, not in the line but as raiders in the image of the failed Lay force. It was to attack Benghazi, particularly the harbour and supply ships supposedly using it. The error made at Tamimi was to be compounded with hundreds of men hazarded instead of 64 and for no good reason. The Eighth Army was dug in at El Alamein, 500 miles as the crow flies from the port and the raid, successful or otherwise, would be of no benefit to it. Rommel was not using the port as it was pointless to do so when others such as Bardia were hundreds of miles closer to his supply depots. The raid was a 'do something, anything' affair.

The route chosen for the journey in which jeeps and 3-ton lorries were to be used as transports was inexplicable, drawn up as if with the Regiment's death in mind. It stretched for 1500 miles, an oblong with one open end, going south, west and then north to the coast. The ground to be covered took in some of the most inhospitable terrain in Africa, including part of the Libyan silent quarter, a place so desolate that even the

Bedouin avoided it. Lawrence's trek across the Sinai desert to attack the Turks in Akaba – hailed as a miracle of endurance – was in comparison little more than a gentle stroll.

The convoy of 40 jeeps and 40 lorries made a convoy over a quarter of a mile long when on the move, raising so much dust that it could be seen five miles away. It was an obvious target for air attacks. The number of men who took part in the raid is not clear; the official figure was 220, but this does not tally with the transport involved and its carrying capacity. A 3-ton truck can accommodate 15 infantrymen and their equipment comfortably, plus the driver and his cab passenger, therefore the trucks alone could have taken 680 men. The jeeps, with a minimum of two men aboard added a further 80 making a grand total of 760, a figure in keeping with the number of men in the Regiment at the time. Water, fuel, food, explosives and reserves of ammunition had also to be carried and if 20 of the 3-tonners were used for this purpose it would have lowered the troop carrying capacity to 460, but still greatly in excess of the official figure.

The Regiment set out for Benghazi at the end of August 1942 and after an epic journey arrived within striking distance on 12 September. Ten hours later when advancing on the town, heavy fire was encountered coming from newly prepared positions. It was obvious that the raid had been expected. Fortunately the fire was inaccurate, the ambush position manned by inexperienced troops allowing the main body of the Regiment to withdraw to the arranged rendezvous (RV) without serious loss. The futility of large raiding parties had again been underlined. What had been clear to some from the beginning was now clear to all; there was no chance of success and the raid was abandoned.

The long trek back to Egypt began early on the following morning, and from the first it became an easy target for German and Italian planes who strafed at will. The journey lasted sixteen days, casualties mounting all the time with a final total of 29 per cent. Some men died in the strafing and bombing runs, others who were wounded lagged behind and were dispatched by Arabs.

The disaster was almost complete and Stirling was devastated. The only glimmer of hope was that the Regiment would never again be forced into an infantry role, and only days after returning from Benghazi, Paddy Mayne – now Major Mayne – was leading his 'company' of eight against the enemy. His promotion had been rapid and deserved. Stirling was promoted to Lieutenant Colonel at the same time having progressed from being the oldest lieutenant in the army to being the youngest colonel in only fourteen months.

The Detachment was also promoted, officially cited as a regiment and admitted to the British Army order of battle. It was recognition of Stirling's vision and Mayne's practicality and should have been a cause for satisfaction all round; but Stirling was not happy. He brooded on the waste of the Benghazi raid, blaming himself. As an act of penance he threw himself into a period of furious activity losing caution in the process, which resulted in his capture during a recce in Tripolitania in January 1943.

Paddy Mayne took command of the Regiment, his style being to prioritise fighting over administration. This attitude was militarily advantageous but limited his advancement, the result being that his last promotion during the war was to Lieutenant Colonel

1199

208/Officers Gen/l G
H₂ 3 Cdn Inf Div COF
20 Jun 45

Comd 2 Cdn Corps

VICTORIA CROSS
Lt-Col R.B. MAYNE, DSO

1.   My orders to Lt-Col MAYNE on 9 Apr 45 were
to pass through my leading tps when they had established
a crossing over the EMS at MEPPEN, then to penetrate
quickly and deeply into the enemy rear areas in the
direction of OLDENBERG. You will remember that the
fighting was very fluid at that time and my division
was making daily adv of 25 to 50 miles. I did not tie
MAYNE down to routes, and he accepted the task with
enthusiasm and alacrity.

2.   The following day we captured MEPPEN established a bridge and re-commenced the advance. In the
meantime MAYNE slipped his force through and I heard no
more from him for over 48 hours, when my leading elements caught up with him in the area of ESTEWEGEN -
LORUP a straight line distance of 25 to 30 miles from
MEPPEN.

3.   I learned then that his force had had some
severe fighting were out of amn and food and at one time
had over 400 prisoners of assorted shapes and sizes.
They had disarmed the lot, had held about 100 of the
toughest type, mostly, paratps, and had chased the others
back in the general direction of our adv. This had been
slowed somewhat by determined enemy resistance in SOGEL
and along the line of the KUSTEN KANAL.

4.   It is my opinion that Lt-Col MAYNE's spirited
leadership and dash were a most important contribution to
the success of the operations. It was no easy task which
I had asked him to perform.

5.   I cannot produce any Canadian eye witnesses to
his personal acts of bravery as his force was operating
entirely on its own. When visiting his unit, however, I
observed the very marked respect and regard in which he
was held by his officers and men.

6.   In my opinion this officer is worthy of the
highest award for gallantry and leadership.

(C Vokes) Maj-Gen
GOC 3 Cdn Inf Div COF

/fp

Major-General C. Vokes' recommendation that 'Paddy' Mayne receive the Victoria Cross for his
actions on 9 April 1945. Many believed Mayne was worthy of the award, even if the army brass did not.

in January 1943. It also prevented him being awarded the Victoria Cross, although he received his fourth DSO for an action on 9 April 1945 when he attacked a German strongpoint, opening the way for the advance of the hitherto stalled 4th Canadian Division and saved the lives of a number of wounded men. Many lesser actions had resulted in the award of the VC, but the DSO was a clear snub and Mayne was made well aware of the political dangers of not providing GHQ with adequate paperwork.

In 1945 Mayne's lack of attention to clerical work cost him the command of the SAS Brigade, which was given to Brigadier Michael Calvert, an Anglo-Irishman dubbed 'Mad Mike' for his exploits with Chindit Force against the Japanese in the Burmese campaign. His appointment rankled with Mayne though both men were first rate fighting soldiers; they believed in leading from the front and were legendary for their courage on the battlefield. Calvert had also received the DSO for an action that many others would have been awarded the VC for; he had played a vital part in the Battle of Nankan, but had fallen foul of army politics.

Chindit Force had been disbanded in the autumn of 1944, its work completed. Its purpose had been similar to that of the SAS, to harass and destabilise the enemy, in its case the Japanese Army in Burma. Calvert was in London when he got the news – the immediate effect being that he was out of a job. Though the Chindits had served the same purpose as the SAS, the group differed in the numbers involved and the fact that it was prepared for, and did fight set-piece battles when necessary. But essentially it was a guerrilla army, striking at targets of opportunity and then falling back on fortified camps to re-group, ill prepared, in fact, for those terrible set-piece battles. In many ways the officers and a good proportion of the men were interchangeable with SAS personnel. This was noted by the War Office when the need for a new commander of the SAS Brigade arose. Calvert, unaware of this and the momentous events he was to be a part of in the coming year, fretted the rest of 1944 away in idleness. Early in January 1945 and completely out of the blue he was offered command of the SAS. Calvert would prove to be an asset, not only to the Brigade in the short term but to the Regiment in the future when its future was unsure.

The SAS HQ in January 1945 was in Earls Colne in Essex and when Calvert arrived to take command he was struck by what he saw as a lax approach to discipline. Most of the men were idle and those who were not were engaged in poaching or other extra curricular activity popular with soldiers who have time on their hands. Paddy Mayne was the senior officer in the camp until Calvert's arrival and was quite happy with the way things were. He considered that soldiers needed to relax when out of the line and if that included taking a pheasant or two from the nearby woods or keeping the maids from the big houses away from their work, why not? Mayne's easy-going attitude and his obvious lack of reverence for the local landowners – one of whom was an ex-speaker of the House of Commons – worried Calvert. After struggling for some time to influence Mayne away from his free and easy approach to the local gentry he solved the problem (or so he thought at the time) by splitting the Brigade. Paddy was given command of both Regiments – 1 and 2 SAS – taking them back to France where there was a pressing need for their services.

Men of the SAS in training during the Second World War.

The Germans were far from finished and had shown in December 1944 that they were capable of mounting strong counter attacks at the most unexpected moments. The Americans had been taken completely by surprise when, during a snowstorm, the Germans had come out of the Ardennes forest and fallen on them like wolves on a flock of sheep. The attack was only halted when the Germans failed to find the fuel and other supplies stored in the American rear. It was considered that the Wehrmacht might put on a repeat performance but were less likely to do so if harried by the SAS. Mayne would see to that in no uncertain fashion. He had some old scores to settle anyway and would be given reason for others in the days ahead. Hitler's order concerning the disposal of enemy troops captured behind German lines was still in operation and SAS men were dying because of it. The simple instruction of the original order, immediate execution, had by now gone by the board and prisoners could no longer expect a quick death. On capture they were handed over to the Gestapo, and once in their hands there was more time to live but no hope of living. There were rumours of SAS men being kicked to death and even skinned alive.

After the departure of the three battalions of 1 and 2 SAS, one Belgian (French-speaking Walloons from southern Belgium) and two French battalions remained at Earls Colne. The French retained links with their past, designating their battalions the 2nd and 3rd Regiments of the Alpine Light Cavalry (Paras). In spite of the name, both battalions were essentially of the Foreign Legion with Legion officers, headed by Colonel de Bollardière, CO of 3rd Regiment. Bollardière had become famous for his courage at the Battle of Gazala, when from 26 May 1942 the 13th Demi-Brigade of the Foreign

Legion held the southern, desert flank of the Eighth Army. For fourteen days the DBLE threw back every German attack, destroying over 100 tanks in the process.

The strange but highly successful hybridisation of Legion and Alpine troops had taken place in February 1940 when the cavalry regiments became part of the 13th Demi-Brigade of the Foreign Legion formed to serve as the infantry arm of the proposed Franco-British expedition against the Soviet Army in Finland. When the Finns and Russians signed peace terms the expedition was re-routed to Norway where the Demi-Brigade won distinction in the hard fighting around Narvik. Calvert, though unaware of the fact, had been involved with the Regiments on both occasions; he, along with a company of Royal Engineers had been part of the British force earmarked for the expedition to Finland, training for the role with both regiments in the French Alps. In Norway he had again unknowingly served alongside the men he now commanded.

Calvert was uncharacteristically uneasy in command. He did not understand the French, or the Alsatians or Spaniards for that matter, and those at Earls Colne were intimidating in their sureness and self confidence. A week passed before he was able to move comfortably amongst them and then, having become aware of the Foreign Legion connection, asked why there were so many Frenchmen in a military organisation reserved for foreigners? When put right on that misconception another arose when a garbled account of the exchange was reported to Colonel de Bollardière, causing a misunderstanding and some friction between him and the new CO. It was sorted out fairly quickly and Calvert continued his efforts to come to terms with the Brigade.

By the end of his first month in command he had developed a high regard for his men.

Calvert wanted to get back into action, but was willing to bide his time in order to achieve a spectacular re-entry. He had been studying reports received from his liaison officer with 21st Army Group for three months when at last he saw his chance. The advance of 2nd Army would be slowed if the bridges crossing the maze of waterways in northeast Holland were not secured before the retreating Germans destroyed them. Their seizure would also cut off the retreat of large numbers of the enemy,

Brigadier Michael 'Mad Mike' Calvert.

bottling them up in Holland with little hope of escape into Germany. If the Brigade could capture the bridges the impact would be impressive.

Calvert, convinced that the Brigade was capable of the task, informed 21st Army Group of his intentions. The attempt would be made, the two French regiments attacking, the Belgians held in reserve. The assault force would be airborne, parachuting onto a myriad of targets in sections, calculated to confuse the enemy and protect the attacking force. There were eighteen bridges in the area to be attacked and when one was captured the Polish and Canadian Armoured Divisions were to advance, relieving the Brigade. Calvert was assured by Staff HQ that the advance would take place within two days of success.

The audacity of the plan appealed to every man in the Brigade. Calvert named the operation *Amherst* after a species of pheasant, a barely disguised reference to the poaching activities of the men which had thinned the local pheasant population by many thousands. The poaching had already been stopped several months previously after the local landowners threatened to approach friends in government; the response of the men had been to introduce the word 'pheasant' into every conversation and pheasant jokes became all the rage.

Operation *Amherst* began on the evening of 7 April 1945. At the final briefing Calvert played to the gallery, hamming a pheasant joke. It went down well and the men trooped aboard the aircraft in good humour. An hour later they jumped into the darkness over north-east Holland. Throughout the night they were engaged in savage hand-to-hand fighting over an area of more than 100 square miles. The Germans were confused by the multiple attacks and failed to concentrate enough troops in any of the DZs sufficient to overcome the attack groups. When dawn came ten of the bridges

SAS raiders behind the lines in France, 1945.

SAS men celebrating a victory with a captured Nazi flag, 1945.

were in the hands of the SAS. During the following eight days the rest were secured. 2nd Army now had a choice of eighteen bridges for a thrust into the heart of Germany. It was a triumph.

The promised advance of the Canadian and Polish Divisions on the capture of at least one of the bridges did not take place however. Now, with all of them in the hands of the Brigade there was still no sign of movement on that front. It seemed that the triumph was to turn into a tragedy and that the SAS was to be left in the same fix as the 1st Airborne Division at Arnhem. The failure to advance did not rest with the Canadians or the Poles. They had been quite ready to honour the promise made but had been overridden by orders from 21st Army Group. Montgomery had at the crucial moment halted all forward movement by 2nd Army; he had clashed with Calvert in the past, coming off second best in the encounter and had nursed a grudge ever since. He had been made to look a fool and now saw a chance to even things up.

But Calvert was not going to let that happen. He had told Colonel de Bollardière that he would get support, whatever the view of the matter at GHQ. The Belgian reserve of 400 men was mobilised as soon as it became plain that 2nd Army was not going to move and set out to relieve the French. Opposition along the way was quickly dealt with and contact was made with de Bollardière within two hours. The groups holding the bridges were reinforced and Calvert went on to scout the surrounding countryside. Pockets of Germans were found and disposed of. Then, satisfied that the immediate areas of the bridges were clear of the enemy, he rejoined de Bollardière. Along the way he was greeted by Troopers who, in his absence had promoted him from Brigadier to General and now saluted as he passed, red berets held aloft on bayonets fixed to 303s. A section leader presented him with a fine cock pheasant; the 'General' did not remark on the fact that it was out of season.

Every crossing to the north east was now held by the Brigade and the German forces in Friesland were trapped. It had cost 30 dead and fewer than 50 wounded. On 16 April, nine days after the promised time, the Canadian armour moved up and the Brigade was relieved from the line.

The French and Belgian authorities wasted little time in recognising the importance of the action and honours were showered on the French and Belgian regiments. Not surprisingly, in view of Montgomery's attitude, the action went without recognition in Britain. The French gave authority for the 2nd and 3rd Regiments to emblazon their colours 'Amherst' and awarded streamers to fly from both guidons. They remain today paraded every year, the legend 'Amherst 7 AVRIL 1945' prominent on both flags, and the Amherst Medal was later struck bearing the same words.

2

THE ARTISTS RIFLES

When the war in Europe ended, the Regiment was ordered to Norway to disarm the German garrison amounting to more than a quarter of a million men. Calvert arrived there with just 35 men and set about the task immediately – and with breathtaking speed. By the time the rest of the Brigade arrived he had already taken the surrender of the army and was in the process of taking that of the naval command. When this was done he took possession of 30 surface vessels and 26 U-boats, the Arctic Fleet of the German Navy. It had been the scourge of the Russian convoys for almost four years, sinking hundreds of cargo vessels and scores of their Royal Navy escorts. Many thousands of seamen had gone to their graves in the icy waters between Bergen and Murmansk because of it. Some time after his seizure of the fleet, Calvert, perhaps unthinkingly, handed it over to scratch crews who sailed it to England. He made no claim to prize money, which would have been a share of around £100 million, divided between him and his men. The failure to claim was an expensive oversight.

The Regiment remained in Norway until October with little of note happening. Mayne and Calvert did have a half-hearted set-to during a mess evening that Calvert came away from with two black eyes, and on Allied Forces Day he got two more, if only figuratively, after

The winged sword badge of the SAS.

taking the salute from the Russian contingent instead of the British. Both the Foreign Office and the War Office came down hard on him. The war was over and Russia was now seen not as an ally but as an enemy once again.

Soon after arriving back in England the Regiment was disbanded without ceremony; the 2nd and 3rd Regiments had already been welcomed into the French Army. Calvert had been as sorry to see them go as he was to witness the final parade of 1 and 2 SAS. He had learned a lot during the time he had soldiered with them and had been impressed, if not at first sight, by Colonel de Bollardière.

Almost as soon as the SAS was disbanded there were second thoughts about it. Man for man it had proved value for money in every campaign in which it took part. When this and other factors were considered it was agreed that the disbandment had been a mistake – but the mistake was not easy to correct. In 1946, Calvert, backed by other officers, attempted the correction but achieved only limited success. Times were hard and the country was bankrupt. It was not the right moment to reactivate the Regiment proper, but it could be reformed as a territorial unit. It was in this form that it was re-established on a part-time basis under the umbrella of a longstanding TA unit with the unlikely title of the Artists Rifles.

Calvert – now reduced from Brigadier to Major, his peacetime substantiate rank – had hoped to become Commander of the new unit but was passed over in favour of a more senior officer. It was a disappointment offset by seeing the Regiment up and running again. The Rifles HQ in 1947 was situated in the baroque splendour of Chelsea in London. The new part-time tenants of the barracks soon took over and the Artists Rifles became the 21st SAS Regiment (Artists Rifles) TA.

Peace in Europe meant that soldiers were seen as surplus to requirements, one-time heroes who were now a drain on a light purse and often troublemakers into the bargain. If they must they could do as they pleased if done out of sight, without fuss and most importantly without asking for money. The new Regiment listened to the voices and slipped quietly, unnoticed into the semi-military life of weekend soldiering. In the following years an image was created that stilled the camp jokes that had done the rounds from the time of its beginning. Artists Rifles conveyed a different meaning to the ORs of the regular army than it had to the dilettantes who founded the regiment in 1860.

Gradually the Regiment gained acceptance from all quarters. Veteran SAS men who had held fire at the beginning became enthusiasts. That came about partly because of the expertise of the editorial staff of the regimental magazine, *Mars and Minerva*. Contributions to the magazine were welcomed from all shades of the political spectrum and great leeway was given to the views expressed. Some of the published pieces resulted in positive moves in the structuring of the Regiment – one leading to officer selection from the ranks, a previously rare occurrence. By 1950 the 21st was an established success. In army parlance it had bags of swank and when regulars admit to this when referring to a terrier (territorial) regiment there can be no doubt that the regiment referred to has well and truly arrived.

3

TRAINING THE SCOUTS

Both men were expert trackers and hunters. They moved through the jungle silently; now and again they halted and kept perfectly still for many minutes, listening. The whisper of a carefully moved branch or a lessening in the tempo of insect choruses caused them to change direction. The quarry was near and safety catches were eased.

One circled the place where sound had faded, decreasing the circle as he moved, stopping every few yards, making sure that he was still the hunter. He was hidden behind a tree watching and listening when the other man came into sight, an easy target for all his precautions and as good as dead. The hunter waited, knowing that when the quarry moved away there would be a shooting gallery target presented, a back shot. The target moved and the hunter raised his rifle and took a sight on the head and the first pressure on the trigger. A split second before firing he changed aim, a little to the right. When the shot went home the quarry fell to the ground and rolled into the undergrowth.

The hunter took no precautions when going forward to examine his handiwork but there was no vengeful shot from the bushes where the other hunter, who had become the hunted, lay. They were companions playing a game. The shot had been real enough but it was small bore and of low velocity. It had taken a small piece from the earlobe causing a fair amount of blood but was far from wound stripe status. The shot signalled the end of the game and the graduation of the players. One had gained an honours degree and the other had salvaged a pass. The game was the culmination of a hectic schedule of training. Both men were now Malayan Scouts, trained in the ways of the jungle and counter guerrilla warfare.

Calvert was satisfied that his men were capable of taking the fight to the enemy. Many of my comrades were long service regulars, hard and single-minded with no illusions about war, although I and some others were younger, although from the same mould. Our average age was 26, high for a combat unit but not too high, about the same as the Paras Calvert had commanded in 1945. Physically we were also a near

The men of A Squadron before undertaking their jungle training.

match, and as training went on the likeness became more apparent. That was as well, for the campaign we were about embark on would be hard, one of long marches and a brave if elusive enemy to outwit. There would be all the boredom of previous wars but none of the compensations: no medals or quick promotions, no set-piece battles, nothing to lessen the hardships.

The purpose of the training programme was to make every man adept in jungle warfare, quick to act and react, capable of getting a shot off that split second earlier than the other man. We had to be able to track and find without falling into traps set by the quarry. The psychological training that would make the practical training work in situ was not neglected, Calvert repeating time and again that everything was in the head. Know yourself and you will know your enemy. When you know, use the knowledge to master him. Your mind must rule your body at all times. When it wants food and there is none, remember that it can function very well without any for at least seven days. When tired and the body says stop, the mind must say no, go on, control the mind and you control everything.

Our in-country training had a marked effect, adding to our confidence, or as some said our over-confidence. By the end of the training period, Calvert had put his mark on all of us in the Regiment. He also changed our views on training and on the command structure – fluid and open to all. We were not just numbers anymore but important individuals, trained to act as a group but capable of acting effectively on our own. The concept of individualism was advanced by pitting one man against another to increase the efficiency of both.

The main assets of a soldier engaged in jungle warfare are the abilities to track, to move secretly and silently and to react immediately. Those qualities were instilled and were mastered through repetition. The men stalked one another through the forest armed with air rifles loaded with lead shot. The less skilful of the two would be punished for the lack when the other tracked him down and got a shot in. The impact of the pellet was painful, sufficient to speed the learning process without inflicting any great injury. With beginners the stalks were over quickly, a matter of minutes, the men entering the jungle at different points and making so much noise that it was not a case of stalking so much as making a bee-line towards each other. The game ended when a telling shot went home. The recipient quickly became a silent traveller, moving like a deer where previously he had moved like a tank. After a week or so, we became good at it, silent in movement, skilful at reading signs of previous use of ground and quick in the use of personal arms. Some of us even became experts, able to close on a watchful group without a sound, taking them completely by surprise.

The game was popular and of our own volition we raised the stakes, using rifles and ball ammunition in place of air guns and pellets. Rather than hitting an opponent dead centre with a stinging pellet, the hunter aimed to miss, although nicking the ear was seen as a hole in one. Serious wounds were frowned upon. They would have to be explained and might put an end to the sport. In time the game became a means of settling disputes, a non lethal duel. The end of a duel was the end of the matter that had brought it about, a perfect way of settling arguments which if left unresolved would have caused ongoing problems. The contests were also a means of fostering mutual regard.

Demonstrating 'proper rifle use'.

Calvert was a past master in the use of explosives, and in the early months of 1951 he passed his knowledge on to A and D Squadrons and elements of B Squadron. Many of my companions became almost as expert as he was, learning to set booby traps of such intricacy that when it came to disarming them they were in constant danger of blowing themselves up. Those fully expert in the art sometimes made use of it in unorthodox ways. One prankster concentrated his activities on the cookhouse, spiking the coal supplies with just enough PE to provide a very satisfying fireworks display when the duty-cook lit the fires. The explosions were harmless, but yielded an unintentional improvement in our meals, as the cooks wrongly concluded that the pyrotechnics were criticisms of their culinary efforts. It was an excellent example of the benefits arising from the proper placement of explosive substances.

Boating was one of the most useful skills taught during training. Malaya is criss-crossed with rivers and streams, ideal for speedy and easy movement of men and supplies. Most of the waterways are shallow but navigable in flat bottomed boats. Rubber dinghies are ideal for the purpose and were our chosen craft. Some of us became so adept in their handling that they were capable of taking one fully laden upstream even though the clearance was often no more than an inch or so. The majority of the watercourses ran either eastward into the China Sea or westward into the Indian Ocean, radiating out from the centre of the peninsula like a ribcage. They were highways to the innermost sanctums of the country. Inexplicably they were never used operationally. It was one of the greatest mistakes of the campaign.

At the end of training we became 'Full Blown Scouts' and were conscious of our special status though without a bespoke badge to set us apart, as we wore the red beret of the Parachute Regiment and the winged sword insignia of the SAS. Everyone knew the significance of these, knew of Calvert's long-term plan to reinstate the SAS on a permanent basis in the regular army.

4

THE HOUSES OF PARLIAMENT IN SELANGOR

During the early part of 1951, A Squadron was in Johore, but I and the rest of the Regiment were over 200 miles north in Selangor, a few miles from the state capital, Kuala Lumpur. Our camp at Dusun Tua was well sited with accommodation for about 300 men, half in tents and the rest in atap and timber barrack rooms. It was a pleasant place to be but tended to lose its appeal if too much time was spent there. Boredom is the lot of the soldier and is not ameliorated by beautiful settings. At such times any distraction was welcomed, and pay days became events. Pay parade was a prelude to a festive evening of drinking, either in the canteen or al fresco around the water tanks; these were well away from the barrack rooms, an ideal place for convivial gatherings. In either place the beer was the same – Tiger, brewed in Singapore and in view of its strength and bite, aptly named. Four bottles were enough to render the uniniti-ated into deep unconsciousness and six guaranteed total amnesia in the most seasoned toper. It was customary for those gathered to tell tall tales, which led to the drinking spot being named the Houses of Parliament.

The tanks were also the centre for aquatic sports even though the water was warm and slightly sulphuric. Everyone took to it at one time or another, voluntarily or oth-erwise. The venue was also popular with monkeys and mynah birds; the monkeys soon accepted us as larger, pinker versions of themselves. The mynahs became very tame, taking food from our hands, and also, rather disconcertingly, words from our mouths. The mynah's skill at reproducing sounds alarmed some troopers at first; it was odd to hear a string of choice insults rendered in a gruff voice to discover that they came, not from the mouth of the SSM but from a bird no bigger than a mistle thrush.

The monkeys came from the nearby forest and after a few weeks they grew rela-tively tame. One in particular became especially fond of human company and took up residence in the camp. He was named Felix for his resemblance to the cartoon cat, and was a monkey with a mission in life, de-fleaing. He had a compulsion for it particularly when pink primates were available for servicing. The only drawback was his belief that

The 'Houses of Parliament'
gather at the water tanks.

his clients could understand every syllable of his endless chatter and when there was no return chat he got very annoyed. He would let this be known by tweaking the ears of the silent ones and only when the expected response was made would he turn his attention back to the head, the only refuge for fleas he recognised on his near relatives.

Spending hours around soldiers seemed to have a similar effect on Felix as it has on many civilians: he began to drink. At first it was the dregs from discarded bottles but soon he could only be satisfied by downing the contents of a pint bottle of Tiger – Carlsberg was also available but he would not have that as it came in smaller bottles. In spite of his addiction he was a civilised toper, taking an hour to sup his pint, doing so in tasteful sips. He would then fall quietly to sleep. When he woke, usually two hours later, he would yawn, stretch, and climb the nearest tree, roost, fall to sleep again and almost immediately fall to the ground. Aware that falling from such a high point would eventually be the end of Felix, some of the men realised that something had to be done. They stopped giving him bottles, but somehow he still managed to get his hands on the hard stuff, and the falls continued. In the end his beer ration was reinstated but with the precaution of placing him inside a box after his drinking session. The treatment was not to his liking but he had to put up with it.

Soon after our arrival the dogs came, strays that attached themselves to the Regiment. They were also fond of swimming in the water tanks but as the monkeys believed that the water was their preserve and that of their close relatives – they paid no heed to the claims of the birds – the dogs were not welcome. When the dogs took to the water for the first time the monkeys were enraged and set about devising ways and means of getting rid of them. Unlike dogs they can swim underwater and made use of this skill to mount submarine attacks against the canines. From then on when-

Author with 3 Platoon's mascot.

the rain stopped, wasting a lot of time. It was 7.30am before at last we were on our way. Twenty miles into the journey the clouds returned and the rain began again. On arrival at the jumping off point it continued but had no effect on the mules. They came off the trucks without a buck or a nip, all in good humour, standing like guardsmen as we strapped their loads in place. When heading into the trees the rain lashed their faces but they butted into it and went on without losing a step. They did not like it but did it anyway. The vet had been wrong about them.

As the day wore on conditions worsened. The mules' packs soaked up water and grew heavier, and the track turned into a quagmire. The mules – who in spite of the conditions had been going well – slowed halfway through the journey, fighting for breath. The belly-bands around their middles had shrunk, biting into the flesh and constricting their lungs. When the bands were loosed the animals shuddered, taking in great gulps of air. How long had they waited to do that? My head had been down too long, sheltering when I should have been watching. Now, able to breathe freely again, they stood quietly, water running down their faces.

By the early afternoon, conditions had worsened. The track was now a miniature swamp, two feet wide and many miles long. The mules sank to their fetlocks in it, slowed but not stopped. When they went too deep we joined arms across their rumps, easing them out of the mud and forward, two shoulders to two back legs, aided by Teddy 204. At 3.00pm we crossed a stream and came to higher ground. It was drier underfoot and the going was easier for a while. Then we started to climb. The mules managed alright for a while until the incline steepened into a one in five slope. We managed it with difficulty, the mules could not. They tried, time after time and each time fell back. They made springs of their haunches and launched themselves at the slope. That took them up a little way but when the initial energy was spent they were left stranded on an insecure footing without the purchase to go any further. When they tried to do so their back legs couldn't follow, the fores skidding out behind them, causing them to slide down the slope.

It was plain that they could not get to the top, but the exercise was repeated a few times until the animals stopped trying and huddled together at the base of the hill trembling with exhaustion. After a rest we decided to try them again, and I volunteered Teddy, thinking that if he failed there would be no point in trying the others. When I took the halter he was blowing but game. He faced the slope and I tied the halter back, patting him on the neck, telling him to go on. He did, gathering himself, charging up the slope. His speed took him as far as any previous attempts but no further and he rested for a while, preparing for the next rush upwards. He was readying for that, bracing his hind legs to push up, when the ground gave way and he collapsed, falling back down the slope.

He came to rest at my feet, blood pouring from his mouth and nostrils and covered in mud. The men stood holding the other mules while I looked him over. Teddy was patient, the rain raising a cloud of vapour from his body, blood reddening a puddle of water by his head. I knelt beside him and he raised his head and looked at me. I put my hand on his neck and looked into his eyes. They were clear of blood so there was no internal bleeding. He still looked at me, requesting approval for his try at the hill. I patted his forehead, approval and reward. He shivered when I loosed the harness and removed the pack.

There was an argument over whether Teddy would have to be shot. He wasn't mortally injured but wouldn't be able to carry his load. In the end it was decided that since he was government property every effort should be made to preserve him. This logical reasoning was followed by the more emotional reasoning of one trooper that 'he'll be as right as rain by morning.' Suddenly, in the gale of rain there was a gale of laughter and the angry faces changed. The argument was over. We would get him out.

I got Teddy to his feet and turned him back along the track. The others followed and just before darkness we arrived at a Malay Kampong. The headman was not overjoyed to see us but agreed, after a lot of idle chat, to give us shelter for the night. The villagers were wary of the mules, saying they had not seen one before, but seemed aware of their reputation for nipping and kicking and gave them a wide berth.

Whilst we now had a shelter for the night the mules remained in the open. To make them a bit more comfortable we sheeted them up and they ate their rations quickly,

The author on the outskirts of the camp at Dusun Tua.

quite content, all except Teddy. It was obvious that he was far from happy so I looked around for some food to tempt him, since he had found his rations so unappealing. I pulled out a bag of porridge oats from my pack, a food of last resort as far as I was concerned but a rare treat for a mule. I offered him a handful, which he explored for a while, turning them with his upper lip, sniffing. Then he mouthed them and began to eat. Within five minutes he had eaten the lot, two pounds, and a week's ration and looked at me for more. But there was no more and I offered him hay instead. He nosed that for a while, still hopeful of finding more oats. When the search failed, he made the best of a bad job and ate the hay. Then I put his full service ration in front of him and he did the same with that. He had had his cake and his halfpenny and was on the mend. I left him then and went to my place in one of the bashas. It was crowded but pleasant, filled with my sleeping companions. After tying my hammock I joined them, swinging gently from side to side in the darkness moved by a soft breeze coming through the open door. I drifted into sleep with the sound of rain in my ears, falling harmlessly on the atap roof.

On the following day, wisely keeping to the valleys, the supplies were delivered. We remained with B Squadron overnight and early next morning returned to the road. There the sky was clear and we loaded the mules in bright sunlight. The return to Dusun Tua took an hour less than the outward run, either a following wind or dry road surfaces. On arrival the mules were taken straight to the stable, a stately building, the best in the camp and certainly the largest, 60 feet long and 20 feet wide, topped by a half moon roof of corrugated iron. Each mule had a stall with a 180-degree view. They could look out into the camp or look at each other and snicker to their hearts content.

When all were watered and fed I had a long look at Teddy. He had eaten up and was ready for more, almost fully recovered and I left him to it. Later that night, just before lights out, I went back and found him standing quietly, profiled against the lesser darkness outside. I put my hand on his neck and patted him. He knew who it was and turned his head, taking my arm between his teeth, applying enough pressure to let me know that with a little more he could break it. He was an awkward, self-willed and obstinate animal. I got my arm back and left the stable. In spite of the fiasco at Bentong, I remained convinced that the mules were an asset to the Regiment. The least of them could travel up to fifteen miles a day through the roughest country carrying a load of 150 pounds or more. They were not only the answer to the supply problem but also to that of the evacuation of the sick and injured. If there was a difficulty about their use it arose from the attitude of those who saw them, not just as beasts of burden but also as skilled mountaineers. But why climb? The war was in the valleys. Still, I was ordered to take the other mules out for further climbing training.

Two days after I returned, Teddy had a relapse. I had looked in on him an hour before reveille and found him cast in his stall, lying on his side as if dead. He did not move when I went to him but he was alive, taking his breath in irregular spasms; it looked like equine pneumonia. There were no medicines of any kind in the stable and time was pressing. What about the RAP? It would have penicillin in stock, but I found it closed. I ran an orderly to ground in the mess tent and after I had explained the situation he agreed to help. Ten minutes later I was back in the stable with a phial of penicillin and a hypodermic needle. Leaving sterilisation to look out for itself I filled the syringe and pumped the lot into him. Then I had to leave hoping for the best. I had either cured him or helped him into oblivion. Four hours passed before I was able to return, and I found him alive and sitting up. He took a long drink of water and when I again came back at midnight he was able to take a handful of oats before settling down for the night.

At dawn my patient was up on all fours, ears pricked and tail swishing, and I considered changing his name to Rasputin. By the afternoon he was fidgety, pawing the ground and snorting. He wanted amusement so after putting the halter on I led him out of the stable. We had not gone far when he got skittish, kicking out with his hind legs and peering out of the corner of one eye like an unemployed Madame in a dockside pub. What had the orderly added to the penicillin? We ambled on for a mile or so around the camp and he was as lively as ever. To settle him, I jumped up on his back, figuring that twelve extra stone would cool his ardour. I rode through the camp and out into the jungle and he went easily, enjoying himself.

The ground was uneven and I dropped the reins on his neck, John Wesley style. A mount will never come a cropper if given its head, picking safe places to put its feet. After an hour among the trees I turned him back to camp, passing through the Rhodesian lines, C Squadron. In spite of their novel views on race I liked them, and when one asked if he could get a few snaps of the mule I agreed, pulled Teddy up and dismounted. As soon as I did he took one look at Teddy and asked if I would ride with him, and I obliged. Some of his friends joined us, all with cameras, and their attention was so taken up with us that after a while I had to dismount. It was that or the risk of a swayback in the section.

A patrol group setting out from Dusun Tua. The author stands second from right.

about 100 miles. Along the way it had to be protected and on that particular trip the escort was made up of McDonald, Paddy Boylan, 'Colonel' Cambell and myself.

We left Dusun Tua early and arrived at the depot at 11.00am. While the coal was being loaded we went on a tour of the camp. On the way back to the loading bay we were passing the cookhouse when a row broke out. It involved a group of cooks who were manhandling two Chinese youths, pushing them backwards and forwards, one to another, punching them as they did so. It was an unpleasant spectacle but we watched for a while before deciding that it had gone far enough. The youths were in danger of being beaten to death. We would not win their hearts and minds but could stop what was a determined bid to knock their brains out.

McDonald struck first and a general melee followed. No time was wasted on the niceties and the bully boys were soon in receipt of double helpings of what they had just dished out. All was soon sweetness and light with the exceptions of the two youths. They were still in fear, heads low, hands held over their faces in the expectation of further blows. Two small bags of flour lay at their feet. They had burst and the contents were scattered on the flagstones, spattered with blood. It turned out that the youths had taken the flour from the cookhouse but were spotted before managing to get away with it and had suffered the consequences. As far as we were concerned they had paid for their inefficient thievery and that was the end of the matter, but the cooks did not agree. I spoke to one of them, outlining the limits of my patience, and as I did so one of his companions lunged at the youths, although carefully avoided any actual contact. As we made no response they all went for it, at which point we roundly punished them.

The cooks then tried a different tack, screaming that the youths were 'Bandits, they're fucking bandits.' Aptly it was the word used by the Japanese to describe those marked out for death. Things were looking very bad for the youths and we moved closer to them. If we could get them to come with us they would be safe; not completely so but safer than they were at the moment. McDonald put his hand on the shoulder of one, to reassure him, gain his trust and get him to go with us to the truck and comparative safely. If he went, the other would follow. When the boy felt the touch on his shoulder he took his hands away from his face and looked sideways at McDonald. His fear appeared to increase, and looking at McDonald I could see why. McDonald was a big man, over six feet tall weighing close on 14 stone. He was unshaven, there was anger on his face and he was armed. I looked at Boylan and Cambell and saw the same. They were not a reassuring sight to the frightened boys and they cowered away. That encouraged the cooks and they chanted louder, more shrilly.

McDonald swore at them expertly, describing their parentage, the current activities of their wives in England, their final destination and their immediate fate if they continued to shout. The boys moved towards their onetime tormentors; it seemed they preferred the devils with shaven chins to those who were unshaven. But we did not give up on them. Boylan spoke to the quietened cooks in his soft reassuring drawl. 'These fellows,' he said, pointing to the youths, 'they're

A Malayan Scout winning hearts and minds.

F.G. 'Paddy' Boylan.

not bandits, just hungry kids. Look at them.' Both youths were painfully thin, their arms and legs like plasterers' lathes, the skin on their bare chests hanging like sheets of parchment. This appeal to their better nature seemed to anger the cooks, who began to circle again, intent on becoming a lynch mob.

We closed around the youths, taking their arms, trying as gently as possible to lead them away to safety. But they didn't want to leave. They cowered away from us and began to wail. The cooks, still silent, came closer, forming a circle around us. McDonald didn't like that and took hold of one of the youths and moved forward to break the circle. But the youth held back, leaning away from him, terrified. McDonald jerked his arm but he braced his legs and stopped any forward movement. We all tried, again and again to get them to move but they would not. I admired them for this; they were not, in their eyes anyway, lambs for the slaughter. And then I was sorry for the way they saw us; if we did use force their view would be confirmed, if only for a little time. Yet I could carry both of them away easily, one under each arm. That wouldn't be much force, but it would be force. For myself I wanted them to come with us willingly.

Their reluctance to move increased the confidence of the cooks, and the Corporal, now on his feet if not fully recovered from McDonald's jab, ordered one of them to bring the Regimental Police. At that Boylan got very annoyed and seized him, a hand on each side of his neck and shook him, swearing, the words pacing the shakes.

'You fat, overfed, under-worked bastard. Why did you send for them?' The Corporal was unable to answer, his head moving too violently. Boylan shouted at us, 'Don't just stand around, get them out of it!' We moved quickly, McDonald handing his rifle to Cambell and dragging the boys out of the circle.

We parted a way for him and he was almost clear when the police arrived. There were a lot of them. McDonald bluffed,

'It's OK we're taking them back to Dusun Tua for interrogation.' He was good and the provost sergeant believed him but was reluctant to let two dangerous guerrillas out of his hands without recognition of his part in their capture.

'You can do that here.' Check, but still something. McDonald had another try.

'Yeah, that would be OK if we had an interpreter but we don't and if we're to act on any information they have we need them at Dusun Tua.' That caused the

The author stands (on right) with regimental police, outside a camp.

provost to hesitate and McDonald threw in what seemed to be the clincher, 'We'll get them back to you as soon as they've been questioned.' This didn't work and gave the provost a little more time to think. He had two prize catches and wasn't going to let them go easily.

'If you want to ask them anything you can do it here; we have an interpreter.' McDonald said nothing and the provost beckoned to the two boys, who went to him gladly. At best they would be tried for stealing from a military establishment and they would go to prison for many years. If they could be tied in with the insurgents it would mean the gallows, death at the hands of Pierrepoint the scientific hangman, who had been busy in the Colonies and British protectorates since 1946, not only hanging the natives but the occasional soldier as well. As I watched the two youths going so quietly to the guardroom I had to admit we had rather failed to win hearts and minds in this encounter. We walked back to the coal bay in silence. It was 11.30am. We had been in the camp for 30 minutes. On the journey back to Dusun Tua the silence remained, then, with only a mile or so to go, Cambell put words to our thoughts. A situation had arisen and it had been badly handled. That was generally agreed. We had been bested by cooks, RPs and a pair of scarecrows. It was not a happy state of affairs.

7

CRIME AND PUNISHMENT

It was always Captain Edward Peacock and Sergeant 'Jock' Sutherland. Peacock wanted it that way and Sutherland went along with him. Because of them guard duty at Dusun Tua in the summer of 1951 was no longer just a matter of guarding the camp but one requiring dress sense and diplomatic skills as well. Prior to June it had been different; it had been carried out properly but without unnecessary frills. Peacock and Sutherland disapproved of our bohemian ways, hankering after the ritual of sentry duty in England. Well turned out clothes racks were preferred to scruffy if efficient sentinels and one way or another clothes racks we would be.

To help things along 'the Stick' – an award given to the smartest man on the guard detail – was introduced. Having received it a soldier was excused the next guard duty. For a while the idea worked and the guard details turned out like tailor's dummies. Uniforms were starched, webbing was polished to a deep black shine – the sales of

Malayan Scouts at ease outside their camp.

cherry blossom boot polish soared – and brasses were burnished to a brightness that was dangerous to the eyes.

The ceremony of the stick had only been in operation for a week when we decided that it was undemocratic and did something about it – we designated the winner. The orderly officer of the day was not told about the change and continued to award it to the smartest man on the detail – his companions having already ensured who that was to be. It was easy to arrange. He was loaned the best boots, the finest webbing and the most highly starched JGs while the rest of us reverted to our bohemian ways, infuriating the orderly officers generally and Peacock in particular.

He above all others was the bane of the guard and when he was orderly officer the night never passed without incident. During the hours of darkness he prowled the sentry beats like a tom cat in an alley peering and prying everywhere. He had the ability to appear seemingly out of nowhere, a ghostly figure in the darkness of the night and in the whirling mists of early morning. He was invariably accompanied by Sergeant Jock Sutherland. The Captain and the Sergeant were kindred spirits, wandering the camp perimeter for the ruin of sentries. When challenged there was always cause for complaint and Peacock always prefaced that with a question, 'Why did you challenge?'

That was an easy one and we could give the stock reply 'Because it is my duty to do so.' That would be enough to settle the matter for most, proving that the sentry was alert and at his post, but it was never enough for the Captain. 'Did you recognise me before you made your challenge?' That was his tricky back hand shot. Yes and it was wrong, no, and it was wrong. Most of us when on sentry duty knew the Captain well and humoured him by saying 'Yes.' That gave him the opportunity to say 'If you recognised me you should not have made a challenge. You are not aware of your duties,' putting him in a good humour for the rest of the night, which with a bit of luck would last until the guard was stood down.

In spite of his novel ways there was some regard for the Captain and that, as one particular event demonstrated, was just as well. It occurred at a meeting of the Houses of Parliament round the water tanks when a young soldier, new to the Regiment, made a complaint against him. He had suffered a particularly harrowing night of guard duty subjected to the Captain's acid wit at every turn. Now he wanted something done about it, something drastic and put a proposal which if acted on would dispense with the Captain's services on a permanent basis. Fragging was not unknown, but most of those at the meeting were surprised at such an extreme view on what was little more than an extended example of the Captain's usual game of Trooper baiting. Some laughed, refusing to take it seriously, but in the end a vote was taken, amended by bracketing the Captain with Sergeant Sutherland, for one could not have one without the other. The proposal was lost by three votes, proving the wisdom of adding the Sergeant's name. Without it Peacock would undoubtedly have gone the way of all flesh. The kindred spirits had been saved and continued to haunt the camp and surprise dozy sentries. It would not have been the same without them.

Sergeant 'Jock' D. Sutherland.

Peacock was an officer of the old school and outward appearance was important to him. If the stock of a rifle was well polished and the barrel clean he was content – but not all the time. He was consistent in inconsistency. One morning, an hour before stand down he inspected the guard and complimented the men on an excellent turnout. An hour later at the stand down proper he gave all of them extra parades for the same appearance. He treated us like errant children which did nothing for his popularity. Some men were so enraged that they were all for calling another vote on whether he should go or stay, Calvert was absent, having left for Johore a few days earlier, and was barely out of sight before his way of doing things was put aside. Others it seemed had better ideas on how to run the Regiment and how we were to be disciplined; they didn't think that us having minds of our own made us good soldiers – not their type of good soldiers anyway.

This attitude meant that the ethos of the camp became one of overbearing authority and the enforcement of petty regulations. By the middle of July every cell in the camp guardroom, which had rarely been used before, was full. None of those in custody were there because of any serious matter, the slightest infringement of KRRs was enough to warrant close arrest. The results were ludicrous; by 23 July most of my Troop (16 Troop) were inside for what amounted to little more than high spirits. McDonald was the exception as he was doing seven days for an infringement of dress regulations. Burnett and the 'Colonel' were under close arrest and awaiting trial because of a little horseplay in the mess tent. Hogan was with them for having the impertinence to question the sanity of the person ordering the arrests.

I paid them a visit on the first evening of their detention. They were not in the best of spirits, seeing themselves as martyrs to the new order. The cells were full to overflowing with those of similar mind, all of them cynical about the methods used to put them there. After leaving the guardroom I decided to try and do something about it and on the following day had a word with Sergeant Sutherland, who was responsible for the detention of some of the men from 16 Troop. I made it plain that I wanted them out but Sutherland wasn't particularly impressed, so I persisted, arguing the point and keeping my voice low; there was no sense in attracting an audience. Unfortunately my calm demeanour made him think that I was afraid of confrontation, his view being that an argument could only be carried out in raised tones, and fairly soon the discussion developed into a shouting match.

It was still going on when Captain Peacock appeared out of nowhere. He wasted no time enquiring into the ins and outs of the matter and I was immediately charged with insubordination and placed under open arrest. This made the whole situation in the camp even clearer, as I had been placed on a very serious charge and left at liberty whilst others, charged with petty offences, were in custody.

Two days later I was on orders to answer the charge before Major John Woodhouse, the CO of D Squadron and ACO of the Regiment, but it was just a matter of form. The offence was too serious for him to deal with and would have to be sent further up the ladder. The Major knew this but still listened to what I had to say, taking it all in. My version of the event would now get an airing in the mess and that would probably help me at a later date. It would also present a worm's eye view of what was going on in the Regiment to those who should but did not know. It might even give food for thought to the ACO. He was the next rung of the ladder and it would do no harm if he knew my side of the story before he listened to it officially. That would be in the following week, Woodhouse making an order to that effect. I would now have to convince the ACO that my action was justified and proper. If I failed he would have no alternative but to send me for trial by court-martial with the prospect of many years in the glasshouse if found guilty. I consoled myself in that event with the thought that things could have been worse; the death penalty for insubordination while on active service had been abolished some years earlier. Still, trial by court-martial is a chancy thing. I could not be sentenced to death, but that still left the Court a lot of leeway and without the need for the absolute proof of guilt. In such a situation they tended to find guilt and impose sentences not because of any worth in the prosecution case but for reasons of policy and sometimes because of personal prejudice. Many officers throughout the army in Malaya, from which the members of the court would be chosen, had reasons to be at odds with the men of my regiment.

Two days before the charge was to be heard, I and the rest of D Squadron was ordered to Johore to reinforce and aid the withdrawal of B Squadron from the forest around Labis. It had suffered heavy losses through injuries and disease and was now seriously under strength, unable to withdraw in good order without help. We were out on patrol when the message arrived and returned to camp immediately. On arrival it was a pleasant surprise to find that Brummy Burnett and the other prisoners from 16 Troop had been released. We celebrated with a bottle of Carlsberg lager, each man getting a mouthful. We would have liked more but one was as much as funds allowed. The release of the prisoners had a good all-round effect on the Squadron.

Nobody had been happy about the business knowing that the men had been locked up without good reason.

We left Dusun Tua for the journey south at 8.00pm on 3 August 1951. There was a long way to go and enough trucks were provided to allow room to stretch, an unexpected treat. Our convoy arrived in Labis at 4.00am and remained for an hour. As always the time was used in drinking tea and talking. At that time in the morning the best yarn spinners remained silent leaving the field clear for the second division. Hogan topped that, specialising in twice-told tales, making himself the central character in all of them. Hogan was a long service regular with the irascibility of a billy-goat and the manner of a Spanish grandee. He had introduced himself to me some months previously when I was in the mess tent carrying my dinner on a fairly hot plate and looking for somewhere to sit. The tent was crowded and as I passed his table I had the misfortune to nudge his eating arm just as he was putting a fork full of food to his mouth. The nudge caused the fork to miss his mouth and prod his upper lip instead. That did not please him and he was on his feet in an instant roaring like a moose in rut. He had no sense of proportion. As soon as he was upright he took my plate and emptied the contents onto the floor. Then he asked me how I liked that and in the event that I didn't what did I propose to do about it? I didn't like it and would have to do something but where and when?

The tent was full of fragile looking tables that would not survive a set-to of any severity. I was not concerned with their survival but was concerned with the cost of replacing them. I would be in hock for a year if that happened. It was plain that the settling of honours would have to take place somewhere else. Hogan was attached to the signals section at the time, billeted some way from D Squadron's lines, and after allowing an hour for his meal to digest I went along to conclude the matter with him. When I arrived the place was deserted except for one of the Australian signallers, a small man with a wrinkled olive complexion and an aversion to conversation. When I asked where I might find Hogan he did not speak but tipped his bush hat sideways indicating a tent to his left.

As I went towards it Hogan stepped through the flap, stripped to the waist. He had obviously believed me when I said that I would see him later and was now ready for action. He was an impressive sight, tall, broad and without an ounce of fat on him. I gazed in awe for a while and wondered at my casual approach to matters of such moment. Why hadn't I settled the business in the mess tent? I could have answered him in kind there, dumping his dinner on the floor, then a little set-to and it would all have been over. Paying for damaged tables was not so important now as it had been an hour ago. But it was too late for second thoughts.

He only stood for moments in the tent opening before moving. Then he moved fast, charging in with his head down. I stepped to one side and clipped him on the ear as he went by. It was not going to be as bad as I had thought, not if he kept going in that way, but he did not, coming on again with his head up and his hands in a good guard position.

A Malayan Scout trooper in fighting pose.

We sparred for a while, pinking each other's faces. He was good, my nose was witness to that. Blood ran freely from it, staining my shirt. It was no great inconvenience to me but an obvious encouragement to him, as he was growing more confident by the minute. Then I caught him with a hook to the side of the head. It hurt him and he stumbled back and dropped his guard. I went after him straightaway and caught him again and he went down, dazed but still sensible enough to curl his body and protect his face with his arms. He was expecting a kicking and it suddenly dawned on me that if I was in his situation that is what I would now be getting. But I saw no percentage in that and stood back, giving him enough room to know that he could unlock his defence and get to his feet without fear of being kicked as he did so.

As I waited for him to rise I noticed that the Australian had been joined by the rest of the signals section and a sprinkling of others from the squadrons. If the match went on much longer the Gauleiter might make an appearance and spoil a settlement. That would be to no one's advantage. At last Hogan got to his feet and seemed as strong as ever, coming on and closing. He clinched, holding me with one arm and pounding my ribs with the other. The blows hurt and I broke his hold and moved away. It was no use trading with him at close quarters; he was stronger and fitter than I was. I kept my distance, circling, making him a static target. He was now easy to hit and I made the most of it. The match had to be finished before the audience increased. Two more good jabs into his face, nose crushers. I had him and moved in close to put him away.

He stood his ground and I measured him up for the last blow – but never got it away. He got his in first, right on the point and I fell into a black hole.

When I woke I was propped against a coconut tree and Hogan was offering me a drink from a dixie of water. He seemed pleased when I opened my eyes and remarked

'Ah, you're awake then.' I sat for a minute before attempting to get to my feet. He gave me a hand and I managed it. 'You alright?'

'Yeah.' I was still a bit groggy but that would pass.

'Did you get any grub in the end?'

'No.'

'Come on then, I'll get you some from the cha-wallah.'

Hogan was beginning to surprise me. The whole incident had begun when he deprived me of my dinner and now, having just shellacked me he was offering to make that good. But food was not uppermost in my mind at that moment. I felt as if I had been through a mincing machine and was more in need of rest than anything else. Still it was the best offer I'd had that day so I accepted.

'I could do with something to eat but you get it and I'll sit here for a while.' I was in no condition to go shopping – Hogan could punch his weight and then some. He understood and made no bones about it.

'OK you stay here and I'll get off.' He turned to go and then seemed to change his mind and turned back and spoke. 'Don't sit out in the sun, go into my tent and sit there.' Then he turned again and left.

The fight fans were still present and two of them helped me to Hogan's tent. The Australian joined us along the way and proved that he did have a tongue after all.

'That was a bit of alright.'

'Yeah, pity I missed the end of it.' His face cracked at that and for a second or so it seemed that he was going to laugh but just in time he brought himself under control. I found out later that nobody had ever known him to laugh. When we got to the tent he went inside and brought a chair out.

'Sit there and I'll get you a beer.' He went back in and came out with two bottles of Tiger. He gave me one and I supped it, giving only a fleeting thought to how he managed to keep it so cool and got away with having it in his tent in the first place. Perhaps as an Australian he had special dispensation from Calvert to keep beer on the premises. We were on our second bottle when Hogan returned with the wads and joined us, the Aussie producing three more bottles. He seemed to have an inexhaustible supply and every one was as cool as the first. We sat in the sun and supped the rest of the afternoon away.

7

THE RESCUE OF B SQUADRON

After reaching the top of the hill we rested. When Trooper McDonald had enough breath he eased off his pack.

'It's like carrying a woman upstairs except there's no bonus at the end of it.'

We had left Labis at five that morning and were in the jungle an hour later, on our way to find and bring home B Squadron. It had been raining for some time and it continued as we went into the trees making the going that bit harder. We carried only two days' rations, hopefully enough to last until we found the Squadron. The extra space in our packs had been filled with explosives, more than we would usually have carried, bringing the average weight to 60 pounds, the rain adding five more. McDonald was puffing like a grampus; perhaps he had climbed too many staircases for his own good. There were plenty of hills in front of us, all higher and harder than the first, each a cascade of water.

As the day wore on the rain intensified. The forest, usually a babel of sound, was still except for the grunts of exhausted men and the thrashing of rain on our faces. We marched and climbed for ten hours. After the first two no one spoke during the rest periods; we had no breath to do so. At the end of the day most of us slung our hammocks and fell into them, but some were too exhausted to do more than wrap themselves in their ponchos and lie on the muddy ground, undisturbed by the falling rain.

The following day was Sunday and reveille was held back until 6.00am and an hour allowed for breakfast, a rare luxury. We marched at 7.00am. The rain had ceased in the early hours and the day was bright and fresh. Again we climbed and descended hills and went into swamps and out. Eight hours into the march a camp used by the insurgents was found and destroyed. Two hours later we halted for the night. It was a good site with a stream nearby, fine clear water flowing at speed, fast enough to be rid of the mud that had been washed into it by twenty hours of non-stop rain. Shoals of fish, no bigger than whitebait, swam in every part of it, not worth hooking but certainly worth netting.

9

TAX, TODDY AND FELIX

Three days after arriving back in Dusun Tua a squad operating in the forest east of Segamat engaged a group of insurgents, killing four of them. The clash was of no significance, ten similar incidents occurring throughout the country on the same day. It became significant when rumours began to circulate that things were not as they had first seemed.

The rumours were malicious, designed to harm the Regiment. It was said that after the action the dead had been decapitated, the heads given to the Sakia so that reward monies could be claimed. It was true that rewards were paid if such deaths could be proved and that soldiers were not eligible for them. Sakias were, and so it was said that they had taken the four heads to the police and been paid without question, later passing the money on to the troopers involved. It was a neat tale and many believed it, including members of the Regiment. It was of course a complete fabrication. I spoke to every man involved in the action on 20 August, a week after the incident and all were adamant that nothing out of the ordinary had occurred during or after the skirmish. They had no reason to lie and I could find no reason to disbelieve what they told me.

It was another slur in a long line of them, intended to highlight the supposed lack of discipline in the Regiment. The irony of it all lay in the fact that severing the heads of the dead was a common practice in line regiments. It was typical that such acts, condoned on the one hand should on the other be used as a stick to beat the Scouts with. Defiling corpses was not one of our many sins and if we had expectations of rewards for such work they were never realised. After all, our prize for the successful evacuation of B Squadron was removal from good barrack rooms to badly sited tents.

A few of us resented the move but our disapproval was directed not against the men of B Squadron but against those who treated them differently to everyone else, a naked display of favouritism. B Squadron had always been seen as different, particularly by the men of A and D Squadrons, they were the privileged few, a Praetorian Guard. The move did nothing to dispel that view, perhaps that was the intention. But while

A Sunderland Flying Boat cruises over the camp at Dusun Tua.

it kept the status quo it failed to widen the gap of difference; we had got to know the men of B Squadron in the previous week and liked them, although there was still a long way to go before they were accepted without reservations.

Soon after returning from Johore the charge of insubordination against me – which I thought had been quietly put aside – was ordered to be heard on 23 August. The admin of the Regiment, weak in every other regard, was a veritable Hercules when dealing with law and order. I was not optimistic about the outcome of the hearing. Calvert had gone south two months previously and showed no signs of returning. There would have been no problem if he had been dealing with the matter. After looking at the charge sheet he would have laughed, balled it up and slung it into the wastepaper basket. Even if the charge was heard there would have been no question of it being sent for trial by court-martial; rather he would have awarded the usual punishment of a fine of one or two bottles of Carlsberg. That somewhat unusual form of punishment was just one of the ways in which he demonstrated the independence of his command. If a Scout had to be punished he would do so without regard to the punishments laid down in KRRs.

A couple of months earlier his policy had come under fire following an incident involving officers of the RAAF (Royal Australian Air Force). They had been invited to a social evening in the mess and were driving over the bridge on the perimeter of the camp to attend it when they were ambushed by seven high-spirited troopers and a corporal. Not realising they were in no real danger, the officers took evasive action and the jeep ended up in a monsoon ditch. The ambush party rescued the jeeps and the Australians and then departed the scene to celebrate their success. Four of them were later recognised and as a gesture to the injured parties, were put on a fizzer. After the preliminary hearings the four appeared before the Colonel who found the charge proven. They were fined, three of them to pay a bottle of beer each and the fourth – who in Calvert's view had been the ringleader – was ordered to pay two bottles. A fitting end to what had been no more than a little skylarking. Alas the Australians did not see it like that and on the day following the hearing they mounted a sortie, flying low over the camp dropping bags of flour on everything in sight. They missed very little, even scoring three direct hits on the stables, which was a little unfair on the mules. The gossip that began after the raid soon reached Staff HQ where more concern was expressed over Calvert's sentencing policy than the bombing of the camp. But it all passed over his head; he was not one to be swayed by chit-chat. Unfortunately in his absence my case would be heard by the ACO – an unknown quantity.

On the due date I paraded outside his office and was marched in by the Sergeant Major, cap and belt off. The charge was read out and then all went silent while the ACO went through the written evidence. I stood at attention and he sat, reading and twiddling a pencil, rolling it like a prime Havana cigar.

'The charge is too serious for me to deal with and you will be sent for trial by court-martial.' He asked me what I had to say on the matter, which surprised me. Perhaps this was my chance to settle the whole thing.

'Sir, I had no intention of being insubordinate, I spoke as I did out of concern for the efficiency of the Troop.' He held up his hand at that and I stopped speaking.

'So you admit to the charge?'

'No sir.'

'You did say that you had no *intention* of being insubordinate.'

'Yes sir, I made a poor choice of words.'

'You have admitted to insubordination without intent in your own words.' He paused and I had time to think that I wasn't doing very well. Soon he would don the black cap. Still I was beginning to have a sneaking regard for him. He was a pedant in the best sense of the word and that appealed to me. I noted his mistake, confusing intent with the act; it was almost as great as my own and I pounced on it.

'Yes sir, but I am not charged with that offence.' That halted him and for a moment I thought he was going to smile. He had a sense of humour and a good regard of what was right and what was not. We both knew it was an open game again.

'So you will go on to contest the charge?'

'Sir, I would prefer you to hear the charge.' He appeared to like my acknowledgement of his perceptive abilities and his face cracked a fraction again. He was enjoying himself.

'In that case and if the finding is against, will you accept my punishment?' 28 days in the lock-up was the maximum he could award and that compared very favourably with the years I could expect if guilt was found by court-martial.

'Yes sir, I will accept your punishment.' The game was swinging my way again and I grew confident.

'Guarding' a bridge.

The prosecution evidence was to be given first but Captain Peacock and Sergeant Sutherland had not turned up for the hearing. In their absence the ACO read transcripts of their evidence aloud and then it was my turn. I went through the sequence of events leading to the charge exactly as I had done with Major Woodhouse but when I came to the shouting match I slowed the delivery.

'Yes, voices had been raised but by all concerned, I had to raise mine to be heard over theirs. I did not tell Captain Peacock to get fucked. I did not refer to Sergeant Sutherland as a sheep-shagger. At no stage did I demand the release of certain prisoners. I did ask if they could be freed. I was not speaking on my own behalf but for the benefit of the Troop. There was merit in my request and that was shown a few days later when the men were released. Discussion, even if loud and heated, is not an offence when all parties are similarly engaged.'

'Is that all?' He was pretending to be serious and looked at me as if I might, with a little more effort, have managed to trot out a far better tale.

'Yes sir.' He contained his disappointment at that. I'd got to know him well in the past twenty minutes and was not surprised by his disposal of the case.

'There is a doubt here and I'm giving you the benefit of it. Case dismissed.'

The Sergeant Major was amazed and the ACO twisted his lips, looking pleased. The Regiment had got lucky again. If Calvert didn't come back we had a man in his place from the same mould. That night the Troop drank to his health and success.

Malayan Scouts fell a tree in the thick jungle.

Later that night a rainstorm flooded our tents, as I discovered when I awoke to find water almost level with my mattress. In the morning everyone was digging drainage ditches but no matter how much we dug it had no effect and the water remained. Then Trela, who had sat on his bed while the excavators went about their work, took a hand. He left them digging and cleared a blockage in the monsoon ditch and the water disappeared as if by magic.

Later that morning we had a delivery of mail and I received a very interesting looking buff job neatly typed with my rank and name from no less a person than His Majesty King George VI. Was it an offer of a job at the palace? A knighthood in the new years honours list? The possibilities were endless. I gloated over the impressive initials boldly emblazoned on the front of it – OHMS. No chance of mistaking the sender. How did King George find the time to write to me and who had given him my address? Prince Philip perhaps. I had spoken to him some years before when his ship docked in Cyprus, but we hadn't exchanged addresses.

At last I decided to see what I was being offered in the way of royal favours and carefully opened the envelope. Maybe it was just an invitation to a royal garden party. Then I spread it out and found that it wasn't from George after all but from a chap called Lionel. Lionel was not offering me anything, not even an invite to afternoon tea, but demanding that I send him a very large sum of money at the very earliest opportunity. He promised dire consequences if there was a failure to comply and if I was tardy in doing so his demand would be increased. Suddenly I was all a twitter and my hands were trembling. I was in the clutches of the Inland Revenue. The sum demanded would take care of my pay at the present rate for the following 30 years and the interest on the unpaid capital would take me comfortably into the year 2011. Would I live long enough to pay it?

It seemed the only reasonable thing to do would be to resign from the army and take up a fresh life as a gold prospector. In was the only way I could see of paying Lionel off in the foreseeable future. It needed a great deal of thought but in the end I compromised and decided to return Lionel's letter plus the forms he had enclosed but minus the money demanded. Before putting the demand note in the reply envelope I showed willing by writing across it a comforting note. 'Dear Lionel I would love to help you in this matter but funds are low at present and I have therefore to reject your request for same.' I signed and dated it and then had a pang of conscience. I could imagine Lionel sitting in his drab office waiting anxiously for news from the Orient and then, when at last it arrived, disappointment. I didn't know him but could not bear to think of him suffering when he read the note, so I added a postscript: 'Good hunting elsewhere.' A nice touch, very compassionate.

It was just after adding the PS that I noticed the memo on the demand note stating that tax declarations by military personnel under the rank of lieutenant had to be returned via Company Offices to be checked by an officer before dispatch to England. That put the cat amongst the pigeons but there was nothing I could do about it except hand it to the Squadron clerk and keep my fingers crossed.

Major J.M. Woodhouse (front row, left) with the officers of the newly designated 22 SAS. Captain Peacock stands in the back row, fourth from left.

I'd just left the office after delivering it when a runner pounded after me with a message. Would I mind returning, Major Woodhouse would like a word. When I went into his office he had the tax demand in his hands and a testy look on his face.

'Do you seriously intend that this form be forwarded?' He waved the paper vigorously under my nose. I decided to go legal.

'It is an offence not to return it.'

'So you want it to be sent off?' He had decided to misunderstand.

'Sir.'

'Right then it will be sent but I suggest that you request a fresh form and fill it in properly.' Did he mean that I should send them a postal order for X number of pounds? I had to straighten him out on that one.

'Sir in my view the form is properly filled in and I see no reason to send for another. If I did the tax office would assume that I do owe them the money and am able to pay it.'

'Can't you pay it?' He was serious. 'Don't you have private means?'

'No sir, I cannot pay and feel that the demand was misdirected. It is obviously meant for someone else.'

'But there is no one in the Regiment with the same name as yours and if it was not meant for you, why did you fill it in?' That was a good return, game to him.

'Sir, I still say it was not meant for me,' Woodhouse was now in his element and prepared to bring me down in flames. The Squadron clerk was hovering at his elbow for some reason and when he nodded his head I knew why, the clerk placing a sheaf of papers before him. They were my army documents and he scanned them speaking as he did so.

'Now let's clear up identities. You enlisted at Westminster and were a student at the time – at Westminster School. Ah, you were in the Army Air Corps, what rank?' He looked up from the papers.

'I had no rank sir.' Private is a rank but he wasn't classing it as such in his question. 'I was only a member of the corps on paper.'

'On paper, what does that mean?'

'Sir, the regiment wanted accommodation for me in the School of Infantry and the AAC was resident there. If I was to get a place I had to be included on their muster roll.' He didn't believe me and I had to change tack. 'There are discrepancies in my documents.'

'Yes?' He was willing to listen, interested even and I seized on the chance to straighten him out. If I could get him to accept that one thing was wrong it would be easy to convince him that others were.

'Sir, I did not enlist at Westminster, I re-enlisted at Warminster and I was a soldier at the time not a student.'

'If you were already a soldier what need was there for you to re-enlist?'

'My period of service was almost at an end and I was persuaded to sign on for a further term with the colours.' He picked up the key word just as expected and led straight out with it.

'Persuaded? Were you drunk?'

'All the enlistment party were drinking at the time but none were drunk.'

'Someone, the attesting officer must have been drunk to enter wrongful information on the attestation paper.'

'To my knowledge sir, no one was drunk. If they were my attestation would be invalid.'

'Umm, right then. You're quite sure that you want the form sent off as it is?'

'Yes sir.' And that was that. Outside his office I made a firm resolve to ignore all buff envelopes in the future – other than to direct them back, unopened to the sender with the legend, 'gone away no forwarding address' written boldly across the front. I had got out of an awkward situation neatly but the day had not yet ended.

The nap club met that afternoon and in the match drawing I got the short stick. That put me at the beck and call of the others for the rest of the day. Over the past month or so we had developed a taste for palm wine. The mechanics involved in its production were simple. The coconut which was the staple was primed with sugar to begin the alcohol-producing process. That could be done in situ or by removing the nuts and taking them to a place of safety where they could ferment without interference.

the same, swamps, hills, trees and more trees. Every patrol was a matter of boredom relieved by flashes of terror and the short-lived elation of action. The actions were not important in themselves, drips of water on a stone, but thousands of them added together totalled the war.

Operation *Cartwheel* began on 5 September 1951 when we in D Squadron, commanded by Major John Woodhouse, set out from Dusun Tua to man Clapham, a camp deep in the forest of Johore. It was to be used as a base from which patrols would go out to clear and dominate the surrounding area. We were to be supplied by air enabling it to remain operational for as long as required. Land, the domain of the insurgents, was to be claimed and held, the Squadron holding a fortified position in the midst of the enemy. The idea was not new. It had been used successfully by the French in Tonkin China during the campaign of 1892. The officer credited with the idea then, Colonel Joseph Calliene, summed up the purpose of such places as 'springboards for surprise attacks against enemy strong-points'.

Rations and ammunition for the operation were drawn on 4 September and section leaders were issued with a quart tin of rum 'for use when required'. After the operation, most of the tins were returned to the quartermaster unopened. It said a lot about our hard drinking reputation; we drank, but not when there was work to be done.

The field rations were good: bully-beef, rice and biscuits augmented with tins of exotic meats and vegetables. It was rumoured that they had arrived at the QMS store having strayed from a consignment of K rations on their way to the US Army in Korea, rerouted north from a ship tied up in Singapore harbour. We were glad of them whatever their source. Fuel tablets, part of the field rations, used almost exclusively for boiling mess-tins of water were wonders of housewifely virtue, each one sufficient to boil a pint of water in six minutes flat. It was the favoured measure of the favoured brew of the Scouts – tea.

As well as food and ammunition we each carried a medical kit containing phials of morphine and quantities of tablets, mepachrin, poludrin and salt. Each had a specific purpose, poludrin was to ward off malaria, mepachrin to purify water and salt to prevent dehydration, the main killer in the forest. The air temperature in Malaya is a constant 90 degrees Fahrenheit and that added to a high humidity created an atmosphere similar to the stokehold of a coal-fired ship. In such an environment the mere act of raising the hand to wipe sweat from the face was enough to cause greater sweat. When carrying a 60lb pack through the jungle we lost half a pint of water in every hour. In spite of that the body continued to function if the salt, lost with the water was made good, and the salt tablets did that. Water was a constant problem, either too much or too little and over a period we developed a way of dealing with it. Throughout a day's march we took salt tablets regularly and drank the contents of our water bottles – just over a pint. Then in a country of water, though it was never in the right place at the right time, we went thirsty. At the end of the day and if lucky enough to camp near a stream we drank huge quantities, much as birds do after roosting in darkness throughout the 12-hour jungle night.

The high humidity of Malaya meant that whenever possible the Scouts would get out of official uniform.

On every operation we were allowed a choice of personal weapons. The selection wasn't great but included sub-machine guns, carbines and the dependable 303 rifle. In the days preceding an op those who were thinking of making an exchange tested out the various weapons on a makeshift range near the camp. I had always liked the 303 but on this occasion decided on a change. Having tried a few I settled for the semi-automatic US Army issue carbine. It was light, had a high rate of fire and was very accurate. I would later find that such qualities were not sufficient for the required purpose; it had no stopping power and that lack almost cost me my life. It was a toy rather than a weapon.

Clapham lay 200 miles south of Dusun Tua and the journey was to be made in 3-ton trucks. We boarded them just before 11.00pm on 5 September 1951. There were 50 of us including two Sakias and Kang the Chinese liaison officer. Kang was a major asset to the Squadron, a man of infinite capacity. He was sociable and loved to talk, going on for hour after hour on almost any topic, dispelling the myth of the inscrutability of the Chinese character. We chatted together throughout the journey, though he took the leading role in this. Nothing could stop him when in full flow and when the truck took a hairpin bend a little faster than it should, he went on talking, keeping himself in place by hanging on like grim death to a slat on the fixed bench on which we sat. The roads were so-so but the drivers made them definitely dangerous; it was always debatable whether they would make it round the next bend. Night travel by road is not the best way of getting from A to B in Malaya.

There was room in the truck to stretch but sleep was difficult, every twist in the road throwing men and kit from one side of the truck to the other in a jumble of bodies and equipment. Some saved themselves from the regular jumbles by sitting on the benches at the sides of the truck. Corporal Mick Dillon had a good seat near the tail gate close to where I sat with Kang. Now and again he joined in the conversation.

Dillon was young, about 24 years old and slightly built, thin, with a fresh pale complexion. He looked like a university don rather than a soldier, yet he was a soldier and a very good one, cool, calm and collected – a younger version of Woodhouse. 'Colonel' Cambell made a foursome at the tailgate and we talked through the night. He was 'the Colonel' because he personified everybody's perception of one, with his moustache, a Regimental treasure, his immaculate turnout, his accent pure Oxbridge. That had proved useful on many occasions in the past when soft, melodious and diplomatic sounds were required. It was a voice worth a hundred fists. In a way he was the occidental equivalent of Kang, excelling him only in the telling of fanciful tales. He was in the middle of one of these when there was an almighty bang at the front of the truck and it rocked from side to side coming dangerously close to overturning. Then the brakes screeched and held, steadying it, the locked wheels skidding along the tarmac, throwing us around like dice in a cup. We swore a lot. After an age it came to a halt and we got out, quick as lemmings over a cliff taking up defensive positions at the side of the road. It was 5.00am, ambush time, and we tensed for action, safety catches off but holding fire. In the half-light targets could not be seen and even in the deadly silence could not be heard. When the light came the expected hail of bullets did not arrive and we relaxed. Yet we had been ambushed, not by the insurgents but by the truck-driver, the mechanic responsible for maintaining the vehicle and by those who had authorised its use.

An ambush party in clearing prior to 'moving out', an army-issue Bergen on the right.

At 6.00am we were picked up by another truck and an hour later were in A Squadron's base camp near Segamat greeting old comrades. The rest of D Squadron had been there since dawn and showed great interest in our bumps and bruises, commenting sarcastically about the possible award of wound stripes; did a black eye qualify?

We remained at the base for the rest of the day cleaning weapons, talking and inspecting the camp. A Squadron's version of the SAS motto – 'who dares wins, who the fuck cares who wins' – was still in place. The ORs of both squadrons held each other in high regard, but the rest of the Regiment did not share the sentiment when it came to A Squadron. The men had a reputation for hardness and ferocity that gave a false impression of their character to those who had nothing else to judge them by. They did have a healthy disregard for army vanities but this was shared by the best officers in the Regiment. Everything said about them was based on supposition, their supposed ill-discipline, hard drinking and over-eagerness to fight. The fact was that they were unorthodox soldiers in an unorthodox regiment, which enabled them to carry out unorthodox tasks successfully. They resented, as did many of us in D Squadron, what they saw as a creeping takeover of the Regiment by officers whose intent was to change a successful unit into what was little more than a line regiment. They wanted to soldier while others wanted to play. Calvert had made them a self-confident elite and that was what they wanted to remain.

Those who did not value their abilities claimed that insubordination was second nature to half of the men in the Regiment, especially those in A Squadron. The thinking was that imposing increased discipline would make the men more pliable, a toy safe to play with. It was claimed that officers were being killed by their own men, a lie retold for the purpose of discrediting the Regiment, and it was repeated so often without denial that in time it was accepted as fact. While on occasion a bullet was put over the head of an officer – it even happened to the Old Fox – there was never intent to kill. It was a way for the men to test their leaders and was accepted as such. The one incident which perhaps could have been seen as an attempt at killing an officer occurred almost a year after the original lie surfaced, and it did not happen on active service but in the safe haven of Singapore, of which more later.

We remained with A Squadron for 11 hours, long enough to dull the aches of the bumps and bruises received on the road. At 6.00pm we left to set up an ambush on the perimeter of a nearby rubber estate and were in place an hour later.

All had been quiet as we moved through the trees, not a breath of air stirring. It was as if we were on the moon. That changed when we had been settled into position for about ten minutes. A babel of sound began around us, crickets fiddling, bull frogs croaking, only silenced when larger animals appeared, a pig taking its young to root for truffles under the rubber trees. Any creature not usually in the area brought silence, which we appreciated as they were effectively guard dogs, and the noise kept us alert through the night. No one could nod off while the bullfrogs were practising scales.

Waiting on events in an ambush position is not the most exciting thing in the world. There was a view at times, from the blackness of the forest into the lesser dark of the

I set off an hour before dark, travelling light with only my carbine, six spare magazines, a full water bottle and my little bakelite camera. When darkness came I was near the top of Hill 615. It is easy climbing in light order and I had made good time. It was strange to be alone on the hill and without the dead weight of a pack weighing me down and I felt as light as air. The going was slower in the dark but still easy and soon I was going down into the valley. The descent, apart from a fall, was as easy as the ascent. When off the hill and into the denser jungle beyond, the darkness was intense, but I was not alone in it. I could hear animals moving through the undergrowth, but my presence did not seem to concern them. Perhaps the darkness changes things. I could not see them and they could not see me. But did sight make a difference? If I was aware of them they, with much keener senses would certainly be aware of me. Could it be that they only had a fear of man in the light of day in the way that man only has a fear of ghosts in darkness?

Just after 2.00am I heard a new sound ahead of me, ponderous and sustained. I wondered about it but kept going. If I'd stopped for every strange noise heard that night I would not be very far advanced. Then, suddenly I was in the middle of the sound and put my hand out to feel the way and touched living flesh. It had the feel of wrinkled leather, sprinkled with harsh stiff hair. It moved under my hand crossing the track from right to left in front of me and my hand ran along the whole length of its flank. Then it was gone and another brushed alongside and I stepped back keeping my hand out and touched another. I was in the middle of a herd of very large animals. They were not elephants, I had no fear of them, but rather cape buffaloes, perhaps the most savage animals in creation, at least according to the stories I had heard about those in Africa. They were said to have all the negative qualities of man, killing other animals seemingly through whim rather than as a defence.

When I realised this I went stiff with fright, unable to think or move. After an age the first fright went and I was able to think. I'd passed many animals that night and none had reacted to my presence in a hostile way, maybe the buffaloes would be the same. They seemed to be ignoring my presence, and besides, perhaps the Malayan variety were not quite the same as those in Africa.

When able to move my legs again I wanted to go on but was unable to control what I now knew to be an irrational fear and instead of moving forward slowly I edged backwards. When I felt a tree in my back I slipped the carbine off my shoulder; front and back were now protected and I felt secure. I listened to them passing; there was no change in the rhythm of their steps, no pause or hesitation or change of direction. None were going to veer and flatten me against the tree after all. I had been overly protective of myself and had lost a lot of valuable time in the process. I checked the luminous dial on my wrist. It was 2.10am. Clearly my sense of time had been lost in my terror, but yet more time was being lost. Why were the beasts moving so slowly? Would they speed up if I put a burst of fire over their heads? Possibly, but it might be in my direction. I let them go at their own pace. Then all at once they were gone.

I moved from the tree and went on. An hour before dawn I came to the junction of the track leading to Clapham, half an hour from home. It would not be safe to approach it in the dark and I settled down to wait. When the light came I went on my way. Fifteen minutes later I moved off the track and into the trees. Sentries are nervous and trigger happy in the first hour of light and if I was shot the effort of the night would be wasted. But no sentries were posted, which surprised me. I looked into the camp, hidden while those in it were in full view. I could see around 40 men, amongst them Dillon, Dover, Waters, Boylan, Burnside, Cambell, Conway, Jock Smith, Sutherland, Woodhouse, McDonald and Hogan. They were all there and all were vulnerable, grouped together attending to breakfast, watching water boiling, making tea.

I had travelled light but still had enough ammunition to kill everyone in the camp; there was a clear field of fire to every part of it. No one was safe. I took a shot, a photograph of them and then slipped in behind one of the bashas and reported to Woodhouse. He was busy, in conference with the signaller and I waited. I had been walking for thirteen hours, what matter a few moments.

He was not pleased with my report and chewed the cud before speaking. Then he asked for a message pad, wrote on it and handed it to the signaller. He tapped out the message and got an immediate reply. Sergeant Matthews would be evacuated later that day. I awaited some comment from Woodhouse but he remained silent. It seemed that

Hogan, Griffiths, Trela and Corporal Dillon pose in a jungle clearing.

18 Troop was now my responsibility, as I had been forced to assume command, and I expected him to confirm it but he did not. Instead he said that Corporal Dover was to return with me and take command of 18 Troop for the time being. This was a snub to me, who had shouldered the burden of responsibility in a time of crisis, and was belittling to Dover, who would get no increase in pay or rank for the job.

The Squadron was still being run on the cheap, there was no doubt of that anymore. Dover was to carry out the duties and responsibilities of a Captain while remaining a Corporal and I was to remain a section leader but without the two shillings a day that went with the job. It was pure farce. Those who had held the rank and were paid to do the job had fallen by the wayside while those who remained and carried out their duties were neither paid nor promoted. The Mandarin system, destroyed in China in 1949 was alive and well, prospering in the bosom of the British Army. Promotion was a factor that had a lot to do with the morale and efficiency of the Squadron. Already, after only a few weeks into the operation it was at half-strength with only one effective officer. If losses went on at the same rate it would cease to exist by the end of the month. Yet that did not have to happen. The men needed to see their companions recognised when merited and if that was not done it killed any initiative in them. What was the point of doing things if they were disregarded? Fourteen hours ago I had left Murray in command of 18 Troop and when I returned he and the others would expect me to resume command, as was merited. The truth was to hit them hard.

Everything is devalued when done on the cheap and costs were being kept down in the Regiment; frugal housekeeping is a winner with the War Office. A cheaply run regiment equalled an efficient regiment in their eyes and we were going along with them in that fallacy; a miser spending a pound on light to find a misplaced penny.

On the way back to the Troop I made a point of getting to know Corporal Dover. He had been with the Squadron for some time and though I had seen him around had never got into conversation with him. I made up for that on the journey and found him to be intelligent and open minded. More importantly he was willing to accept that others might know more than he did and was willing to learn. Physically he was a big man, over six feet tall and weighing in at about 13 stone, some of it fat; he would soon tighten that up in our company. On arrival at the base I explained the situation to the men and introduced Dover. They accepted him without comment. We remained in the area for a further two days and then, our work completed, moved out to rejoin the rest of D Squadron.

The climb of Hill 615 began an hour after dawn. It was my fifth time on the hill and I was growing attached to it. We went up the easy way and arrived at the top with air in our lungs and miles in our legs. It is the way to be at the top of a hill.

We got to Clapham at 3.00pm and had the rest of the day to make do and mend. I went fishing, as it was the first chance I'd had to do so during Operation *Cartwheel*, and was on the riverbank by 4.00pm. The flood had subsided and the water was now clear and bubbly. It was hard to believe that I had come close to death in it such a short time before.

A rare opportunity to wash in camp.

The fish were there, lively and on the feed and I had bait to entice them to the hook, gutted leeches. They had fed off me and now it was their turn to help in my feeding. The fish liked them, forming a queue to bite, having no experience of hooks or fishermen. I'd banked ten in less than an hour and they were all of a fair size weighing between 8 ounces and a pound. The species was unknown to me but had a look of European roach and in the absence of better information roach they were. Back at the camp I divided them between the Sakias, keeping one of the larger ones for myself and I cooked it for supper. It was good, the flavour excelling that of clean run salmon, beating bully by a street.

On the following day we went downstream to set up another patrol base. The selected area was five miles away and it took us half a day to get there. Near the end of the first patrol from the new base we were resting prior to the last lap when Trooper Ned Murray discovered that he had lost one of his Owen gun magazines. He was certain that it had been left at our previous stopping place and asked if he could go back for it. I thought about that for a while before agreeing. The extra mileage might teach him a lesson on the care of equipment – and the track was well marked so it was unlikely that he would get lost.

After he had gone, we waited. He was in light order and would be back within the hour but he wasn't. When darkness came he was still absent and I knew that I would have to go and look for him. We returned to base and I let Dover know what was going on and then went back along the track to commence the search. The going was not easy in the dark and it took more than an hour to reach our last stopping place and longer still to reach the second, the one where Murray had mislaid the magazine. There was no sign of him but he had to be laid up somewhere near and I called his name out softly. There was no reply and I called loudly, still no reply. I moved and shouted and listened but there was only silence. I kept moving and stopping and shouting until I was hoarse. Then I got a reply, a burst of fire. It was high and no danger to me but I went to ground anyway; no sense in tempting fate.

Secure on the ground I eased the safety catch on my carbine and crawled towards the source of the firing. Whoever had loosed the shots was aware of my position and would expect me to either stay there or fall back. Doing the opposite would give me the benefit of surprise. I moved through the trees quietly and another burst came my way; obviously I had not moved quietly enough. But now I was near to the source of the shots and heard the sound as a magazine was clicked off. The would-be assassin was now disarmed and I could kill him before he had time to re-arm. I was tempted to do so but held back. Murray had been drilled to use arms only when there was a target in sight and it was therefore unlikely that he was responsible for the shots, but one never knew. In any event I held all the cards, the second burst had gone high and my position was still secure. In case it was Murray I would have to be careful as it would not do to kill him. I could not live with that or the thought of the effect it would have on his family when they received the telegram from the War Office.

The author with a 2-inch mortar, preparing for a patrol.

I was positioned behind a tree, in no danger of being hit while my opponent was exposed and vulnerable. Even if he knew where I was it would be no advantage to him, he was in a no win situation and I could afford to give him leeway. I called out, softly. If I got the wrong response I would fire and that would be the end of it. If it was Murray I hoped that he had his wits about him and a ready tongue in his head. The carbine was set at automatic as I whispered his name. There was no answer for a while and then a question came out of the darkness. 'That you Joe?' It was an innocent enquiry but for some reason or another it annoyed me. It was 3.00am and I was tired and nervous but not too tired to bollock him. He listened in silence and when I'd finished remained silent, at which point the penny dropped. I had said nothing when security had been broken on a previous patrol and had no right to say anything now. Murray had known that from the start and had allowed me enough rope to hang myself. Now, all I could do was to put my hand on his shoulder and say, 'Come on Ned let's get back.' He accepted my gesture of fault acknowledged and we started back to base. We made good time, arriving just after reveille and sat together over breakfast, indulging ourselves, drinking tea and eating biscuits as if we had an inexhaustible supply. Murray had already forgotten my harsh words. It was his way.

The Troop remained in the area for four days and then returned to Clapham. Supplies were short and an air drop was expected, and it arrived on time and bang on target. I salvaged one of the parachutes; the silk would make a luxurious cover for my hammock. The field post office had also found us and there was a batch of letters in

Letters from home were of great comfort to men of the regiment.

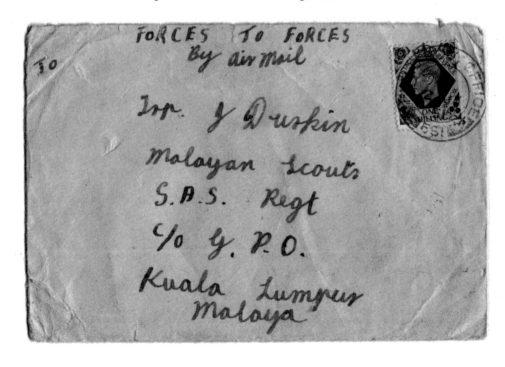

one of the containers, one of them for me. It was from my mother and apart from the letter the envelope also contained something very special, a medal blessed at Lourdes. She had got it for me while visiting France earlier that month. It was the medal of the Immaculate Conception and of great significance to Catholics. Those wearing it would not die before receiving absolution. I held it in the palm of my hand for a while and then removed the identity discs from around my neck and replaced them with the medal. Identity discs are part and parcel of the soldier's persona, issued on joining and impressed with his name, regimental number and religious denomination. One of the discs is red and the other green, the former to be taken from the body if a soldier is killed, in order to record the death, the latter left with him for the benefit of the burial party. My discs would not be required on the operation and we did not have a priest with us – the Regiment did not have one. The medal would be more useful.

What remained of the Squadron was now gathered together at Clapham and after the distribution of the new supplies preparations were made for a patrol in strength. The Squadron was to march together, the first time since the beginning of the op. It was said that we were going into hilly country which did not surprise me. 18 Troop had been climbing hills since early September.

The ascent of Hill 885 was no harder than any other but it did for Trooper O'Brien. He found it hard but still managed to struggle to the top and then collapsed. I was at the rear of the column and on reaching the ridge saw him, exhausted, his kit scattered around him. When I looked at his face it was grey and old, much older than his 36 years. He was thirsty and I gave him a sup of water from my bottle. He had finished his on the way up but still had a raging thirst and was reluctant to let go of my canteen. But too much is as bad as too little and I took it away from him.

O'Brien was an old soldier and it now seemed that he was about to fade away. He had remained in the trade too long for his own good and was suffering the consequences. He was an original, one of the first SAS men. Stirling had given him his breast badge in Egypt ten years before and he had worn it ever since, in Africa, Europe and Asia. He was extremely proud of it. Before the start of that day's march it had been made clear that stragglers were to be left to fend for themselves, but I could not accept that fate for O'Brien. If he was to be left then I would stay with him. The thought of him dying alone on the hill was unbearable and I was angry. Younger men, officers, all with curable diseases had been helicoptered out to safety while an old soldier at the end of his tether was to be left to die like a dog by the side of a road. Besides the inhumanity of it, there would also be repercussions in the Regiment. Men would question why such a faithful soldier had been abandoned, trust would be lost.

Having made up my mind, when the Squadron moved off I remaining sitting by O'Brien. As the last man disappeared the forest came alive with sound and spectacle. Game fowl crowed and monkeys came down from the trees to search for crumbs dropped by the men who had rested on the track moments before. They were joined by a multicoloured bird who pecked in the dirt.

The old man of the regiment, Trooper O'Brien.

After resting for an hour blood came back to O'Brien's face. It was still white but so was mine but his was now a healthy shade, not blooming but improved in colour. I gave him the last of the water and made him swallow a salt tablet. He gagged on it but got it down. That convinced me that with a bit of help he would make it, the salt and water renewing him. There were plenty of salt tablets but both canteens were now empty and if he was to get out safely, water was essential.

We had passed a stream just before coming to the hill. It was a two-hour round trip but I would have to go if we were to have any chance of rejoining the others. I went down the hill in quick time, arriving at the stream in less than an hour. The water was shallow and as clear as a bell, too low for fish of any size but deep enough for shoals of pinkeens, darting here and there. After filling the canteens I took in as much water as I could, sufficient for the rest of the day. O'Brien would need both bottles. I took it easy on the way back up the hill; there was no point filling up with water and then sweating it away to no purpose.

O'Brien was in good spirits when I got back and after a drink got two more salt tablets down. He had now been resting for almost four hours and it showed. Still I was surprised when less than an hour later he said that he was ready to go on. I agreed on the understanding that he dumped his pack; his new found vigour would soon go with that on his back. He agreed and I packed his rations in my bergen, leaving him with a bandolier of ammunition and a rifle to carry and an easy track to follow.

He led off setting his own pace and went well, almost too well, as the extra weight in my pack soon lowered my head and I was struggling to keep up. I couldn't ask him to take it easy, that would destroy his confidence in me and would not do his own much good either. So he went on and I trailed after him like an Egyptian donkey going to market.

Two hours after starting out pins and needles ran up and down my arms, the pack support straps cutting into my shoulders, slowing the blood. It eased when I slung the carbine and got my thumbs under them, shifting the weight. Then darkness came and O'Brien slowed; he was no good without light and I was saved by its lack. In the darkness I took his place, slowing the pace to a point where I could walk with my head up.

Close to midnight I saw a light ahead, a fire. The flames moved, flaring and dying and then flaring again. It was a bonfire and I wondered who had lit it. Not the insurgents, they didn't advertise their presence to that extent. It had to be the Squadron but why the fire? It was about a mile away, the ground sloping away to it. The closer we came the more we could see, a group of men clearly silhouetted against the brightness. We went into the bivouac without notice and I took O'Brien to his section area. When he was settling in I sorted his rations and gave them to him. He was too tired to say anything but put his hand on my shoulder which said enough.

I slung my hammock by the light of the fire and was about to turn in when I remembered the silk parachute and took it out of the pack. It was huge, cascading to the ground when draped over the hammock, a sleeping place fit for a princess, and I rather wished there was one in it. I was tired but not that tired. But I was too tired to go find water, and had accepted that I would have to do without when Corporal Dover left his place by the fire and gave me a mug of tea. It was strong and sweet, an elixir. When I'd drained the cup I got into my refurbished hammock and settled down for what remained of the night.

I awoke at 2.00am in an agony of pain, my stomach feeling as if it had been torn by ragged iron. We must have been attacked, surely I'd been hit by mortar shrapnel! Then I was fully awake and there was no small arms fire, no alarm in the bivouac. The parachute must have caught a spark from the fire and was aflame. I twisted on my side and tumbled to the ground. The folds of the chute clung to me and I tore them away, but it was not alight. Then I touched my stomach, my hands sinking into a slimy moving mass.

The bonfire was still burning and I ran to it, holding my stomach, terrified that my entrails were about to fall out. The men were still around the fire and opened a space for me. In the light I looked down, terrified of what I was going to see. When I saw I laughed. Hundreds of black and red jack ants covered the lower part of my body. They bit savagely, tearing quarter inch squares from my flesh, that looked for all the world like diced vegetables in a can of soup. I was in an agony of pain but now it was without terror, and I tried to remove the ants, pulling at them. But they would not go without their portion, and as I pulled and the body came away leaving the head in the flesh. Dover and the other men around the fire helped, killing and removing the ants quickly. When the last one was gone blood continued to seep from the raw squares. I sat by the fire until the bleeding stopped and then counted the holes on my stomach, finding over 200 before giving up for lack of a mirror to count those on my back. I realised that the ants must have climbed the parachute, which had been trailing from my hammock to the ground, a highway to the banquet. I was off silk for good and on returning to the hammock kicked the chute deeper into the forest.

In the morning I realised that I lost my compass in the night. I checked and rechecked my kit and searched every bit of ground without success and then, when it was almost time to saddle-up, I spied my discarded parachute lying where I'd kicked it during the night. The cord of the compass lay across it and after checking for ants I picked it up. The weight of it hanging from my neck was comforting and I suppose that was why I'd spent so much time searching for it. I certainly didn't use it much for its intended purpose, preferring to use the position of the sun. The compass only really came into its own at night, the luminous dial allowing it to be read in the dark; the power source was promethium, a rather dangerous radioactive element, which was eventually credited with shortening the lives of a number of SAS men. I looked down at mine, bumping against my chest. I was nearly 22 and would live forever.

That day's march went hard and Trooper Eddy Waters eventually had to be evacuated out by helicopter. O'Brien also went and the rations I had carried for him on the previous day were split between undeserving cases. I could have done with a

share but received nothing. Still, I knew that eating every day was a bad habit for a soldier to get into; he might come to expect it. I was pleased to see Waters and O'Brien lifted out to safety, particularly Waters. During our time at Dusun Tua he had made pay nights memorable by his uniquely harsh and unmelodious renditions of bawdy songs. He would commence the concerts after drinking enough Tiger to float a canoe. The beer endowed him with boundless energy and jolted his memory to the point where he had instant recall of the lyrics of every favoured ditty. He would sing these anywhere

An ambush party at ease in the jungle.

but had a preference for the strip of ground beside my tent. The caterwauling would invariably commence just as I was managing to doze off after a hard day. At that point I would rise, dress and lead him to a place where his undoubted talent would be understood and appreciated – Captain Peacock's sleeping quarters. He really liked traditional army ditties.

With the loss of the two troopers I thought that we had seen the last of our ill luck but I was wrong. On the following day we lost six more men and the Squadron was down to little more than platoon strength. But the patrol went on as before, along ridges, down into valleys and on into a swamp. We ploughed through it for many hours, the leeches as always numerous and hungry. I was behind Trooper 'Brummy' Burnett when I saw a leech on his shirt moving upwards at a good rate of knots, looking no doubt for an entrance to the goodies within. On reaching the nape of his neck it continued its journey to the jaw line, eventually coming to a halt on his right ear. It was a tiger leech, a large one, but in spite of that Brummy was unaware of its presence. Having found a place to suit, the leech settled down to eat. An hour later it had doubled in size and continued to gorge. I began to look forward to it exploding. Something had to give. It obviously knew its cubic capacity and just after the hour it arched its body and launched out into space like a free fall parachutist. It fell through the air, spreading its body like a flying fox and plopped safely into the mud. It could now rest on a full stomach and await the arrival of its next meal.

When first seeing Burnett's visitor I'd instinctively checked my own ear and now checked again. There were none on my ears but two were attached under my jaw. They felt like jelly-babies. My probing fingers did not disturb them and they went on with their meal. Later, blood ran down my chest and I felt under my chin again. They had gone and my hand came away soaked in blood. I found that strange, as leeches possess a blood coagulation agent which is automatically dispensed on the completion of a meal, effectively sealing off the flow of blood. Perhaps it only works in less sensitive places. They are strange creatures.

We were in the swamp for most of the day. Moving through such terrain tends to blunt the senses but it is wise to allow for the unexpected. For mile after mile everything is the same but then a step is taken and the boot sinks into deeper water, going on for a further six inches into mud to find firmness. Then the other boot is advanced and goes down twenty inches. Sometimes the mud is almost as liquid as water and the going is easy, like walking through a shallow stream. When the depth varies, going from ankle to the middle calf it slows progress to a snail's pace. And there are dangerous places, pits that seem bottomless. No one gives them any thought unless they have to. The virtue of the swamp is the availability of water; thirst is never a problem there.

We came to firm ground in the middle of the afternoon and prepared for a supply drop. As always the aircraft came in right on time and flew over the DZ on a dry run. Having found us the pilot banked, returned and made the delivery. All but one of the packs came safely to earth, one snagging on a tree 200 feet up. It was lost to us but would give a lot of pleasure to the local monkeys when we left the area. We then went on toward Hill 998. As we neared it the rain started and was intense as the climb began. Water sheeted from the sky and poured down the hill, making it a waterfall. We were all as thin as wraiths after many days of bad food, little water and hard marching, but we scrambled up. The Sakias did not go as well which was surprising; it was their home ground. There were only two of them still with us, one of them the man who had caught the tortoise. He looked frail but carried his pack without complaint. Eventually his companion dropped out but he remained cheerful, even though he had no one to talk to, a brave front by a remarkable man. His forbears had been the original inhabitants of Malaya and remained in sole occupation of the land until the second century AD. Then the Siamese invaded from the north forcing them to take refuge in the jungle, where they have remained ever since. Their way of life has not changed much over the centuries, nor their nature. They are quiet and peaceful with a culture that gives value to all living things, a people out of place in the twentieth century. We had cajoled them to carry loads for rewards that they had no real need for, giving them modern medicine and modern diseases to go with it, curing them of yaws and killing them with colds.

I was half way up the hill when I saw Tortoise Man laying on the ground, unmoving, the support cord of his pack still across his forehead. When I went to him he was conscious but little more. It was hard to ease the cord from his forehead and eventually I had to cut him free. Now he could rest easier and his little grey face smiled at me. We were in the middle of a cloud and his clothing was saturated, but though there was rain

On patrol in the jungle.

all around us he was thirsty. Rivulets of water ran over his face and he guided it into his mouth. But it was not enough and I gave him my canteen. He drank and settled back, contented. I rested by him for a time.

The Tortoise was dehydrated and needed salt even more than water. I had plenty of salt but not enough water to get him back on his feet. The rain had stopped falling around us but went on further down the hill; I could hear it pattering on the canopy. It would be easy to get as much as needed down there but I could not bring myself to go all that way. It could be got by other means, the desert way, condensed out of the air. All that was needed was a surface a little colder than the air around us – the oily, clammy lining of a poncho would be ideal. I closed the neck, laid it in a hollow and waited for it to fill. The Tortoise was taking notice and spoke, pointing to the poncho. I replied, '*panee, panee.*'

Almost everyone in the army understands basic Urdu but I underlined the word for him, cupping my hands as if taking water, holding them to my mouth, pretending to drink. He understood and smiled, nodding, repeating the word, '*panee, panee.*' He had learned his first word of soldiers' English and was pleased about it. I looked into his face so that he would smile again and he did.

While waiting for the water I gave him two salt tablets and my canteen. He was not sure about the tablets but when I raised my eyebrows in query and then nodded my head to say they were good he swallowed them immediately. After an hour the poncho held about a pint of clear, sparkling water. I cupped my hands in it and turned to him. When he saw the water running through my fingers he put his hands together and raised them to his face, a quick learner. I drank the water remaining in my hands and put the rest in his canteen, exchanging it for mine. It was empty, he had drained every drop, but when I gave him his he drank without gulping, swallowing as he should, slowly and with pleasure.

While he rested I took a bag of salt tablets from the bergen, took one out and showed it to him. He had already swallowed two but without being aware of their purpose. If he was ever to return to his family safely that would have to be demonstrated to him, he had to learn. He watched closely as I put the tablet in my mouth, gathered spittle and swallowed, showing difficulty in doing so but patting my stomach, smiling when I managed to get it down. He knew that it wasn't a pleasant thing to do without water to help it on its way but also knew that it was a good and necessary thing. I gave him a tablet and he followed suit. I smiled and patted his shoulder. Now I would show him that they had to be taken on a regular basis.

I took out my notebook and pencil and drew a rayed circle in it, the sun, pointed at the sky and back at the drawing. He nodded. Beneath the sun I drew a line going from one side of the page to the other and split it with a line through the centre, midday. Then I put two salt tablets on each side and two in the centre, stood up, stretched, took two of the tablets from the page and made pretence of swallowing them. Then I moved my finger from the side of the page to the centre: and picked two more up, pointing to the sketch again and then overhead, midday. He nodded again. I put my

We searched the camp for food but only found empty cooking pots. They retained a rich aroma and increased our hunger but there was not a scrap of meat or a grain of rice anywhere. Then I looked at the pig and saw it in a new light. It was no longer a failed killer but a hundredweight of prime pork, more food than we had seen in an age. But there was a drawback; our pangas were blunt from chopping trees and would make messy work of butchery. But blunt or not they were used. At the best of times a panga could not be described as a precise surgical instrument but when it has to be used axe fashion it has no precision at all. Eventually a ham was separated from the carcass along with the liver, kidneys and sweetbreads.

With these as prizes we left the camp to pick up our packs. Then we moved farther into the safety of the trees. About a mile in we halted and prepared the feast. The ham was to be roasted in the traditional manner and fuel tablets were heaped under it, over it and around it. While they blazed away merrily the offal was boiled in mess tins and was ready for eating by the time the ham was ready for turning.

The liver was disposed of first, followed by the kidneys. Then it was time for the greatest delicacy of all, the sweetbreads. They were fine specimens and I was concerned about their division; there were three of us and only two of them. How could they be divided equally? I looked at them for a good while wondering where to apply the panga and then the problem was solved. For some reason or another neither of my companions wanted any part of them. Had they suddenly gone vegetarian? I didn't waste time enquiring and ate them gratefully.

When all the available fuel tablets were used up it was agreed that the ham was done to a turn. All the bristles had gone and the surface of the meat was black. It was not only roasted but perfectly smoked. When the soot was removed the fourth course of the banquet commenced. The ham was attacked in a joint effort, passed from hand to hand, each man taking a mouthful before passing it to the next.

When the outer layer was eaten the inner tended to rareness and by the time the bone was reached it was raw. In spite of that there were only speckles of red on the bone when at last it was thrown into the forest. We finished the feast with water and then set off to retrace our steps to the logging camp. While we walked I considered the day's events.

It was obvious that the insurgent camp had been occupied in the past twelve hours; fires were still burning indicating that the occupants had moved out in such a hurry that they didn't have time to slake them. They had also left valuable cooking vessels and storage jars behind. To move at such short notice meant that they were aware either that the camp was known about or would shortly be discovered and attacked. But how had they known and why hadn't they killed us? They had clearly been unaware of how few we were.

Eventually we realised how we had been found out. When the boy had crossed the clearing through the long grass we had traced his progress by the waving greenery. Clearly he had seen the same movements when we followed him. I had dismissed him as a city boy, but in fact he was clearly an experienced guerrilla and had made a fool of me. Having crossed the clearing he had not continued his journey but waited and

A trooper on patrol in a rubber estate.

Rubber estate patrol.

watched for followers and we did not keep him waiting long, entering the grass almost as soon as he had left it. He had been aware of our presence behind him from that moment. One error had been made for which I would be forever grateful; he had left his position before calculating the number of men following him. Three men move ten feet of grass, a squadron moves 300 feet. The error saved our lives. At the end of his journey he had passed on correct but incomplete information and the insurgents had moved house. They could have ambushed the expected Squadron but had realised that there was nothing to be gained by fighting on ground as familiar to one side as it was to the other. And in any event killing a soldier or two would not frighten the locals. Killing the headman of a kampong would, and without complications.

When we arrived at the logging camp where we had parted company with the rest of the patrol there was no sign of life and I wondered what had happened to Corporal Dover. Before leaving on the previous day arrangements had been made to meet up at the camp 24 hours later. After waiting for an hour I decided to patrol up to the road in the hope that our paths would cross. Along the way we went though a rubber estate, deserted and desolate, hundreds of trees slashed and oozing latex, dripping uselessly to the ground. The insurgents had been busy during the night.

The regimented rows of trees, untended by tappers, presented a strange and eerie sight. The trees represented immense wealth, having created more millionaires than the Rand and Klondike combined. Yet they had only arrived in Malaya in the early days of the twentieth century. But from that time there had been an ever increasing demand for rubber which the modern state had encouraged and was soon dependent on. Did it serve civilisation or was it the other way around? I was trekking through the trees with two ragged companions because of it.

Prior to 1900 Brazil held the world monopoly in rubber and the Brazilians were conscious of the trading power it gave them. The monopoly was protected by laws making it a serious offence to deal in the seeds of the tree or smuggle them out of the country. The monopoly held good until the Court of King James dispatched a new diplomatic representative to the country, Sir Roger Casement. His brief was to get as many seeds to England as he could. He did and they became the progenitors of every rubber tree in Malaya and the Far East.

On reaching the perimeter of the estate we re-entered the jungle, a narrow strip with a stream beyond it, the same one we had come across in a different place on the previous day. We were close to it when a mass of hornets found us. We had experienced their bile on many occasions in the past but their numbers and the persistence shown by them on this occasion was extraordinary and frightening. They attacked in a cloud of fury, stinging bare flesh and through clothing. The stings were red hot needles that did not cool, causing an agony of pain. They stung everywhere, even on the head, the barbs entering through the thick cloth of our hats. I shielded my head and my hands were stung and closed my eyes in fear of being blinded. Then I took my hands from my head to double guard my eyes. We stumbled blindly, crashing into trees and each other and then into the stream. The water closed over my head and the agony

Having a bath, jungle style.

lessened. Then I began to splutter and raised my head to gasp air and they lighted on it, angry as ever and I ducked under the water again. For an age I paid in stings for every breath of air and then they disappeared and the air was free again.

My companions had also taken refuge in the stream and we rose from the water together and looked stupidly at each other for a while and then stumbled to the bank and fell down, exhausted by pain and fear. When the pain eased we cleaned our weapons, one after another. We remained on the bank for a long time, tired out. The pain, now dull, still bewildered and though a watch was kept it was by rote and worse, none of us cared. Then we moved into the trees and rested again.

Beyond the stream we came upon a logged track. The dead trunks stretched away into the distance going east to the road, an easy path and we went along it. It was a pleasant place to be, like a country lane in England. Within an hour we were at the road, busy with traffic. There was no sign of Dover or 18 Troop and I decided to head for Labis. There was a HQ of sorts there where I could report in and use the wireless to get in touch with Woodhouse.

The town was about ten miles away, two and a half hours at 180 to the minute and two at 220. Better to ride. I stopped the next truck that came along. The driver was a Chinese, about 40 years of age, accompanied by his wife. He smiled as I explained what was wanted and agreed to accommodate us. The truck carried a cargo of pigs, pink as babies and gentle as spaniels, but that did not incline me to travel in their company. The memory of my brush with their late cousin was too fresh in the mind. Fortunately the driver's wife had no such inhibitions and willingly gave up her place in the cab and joined Tommy and John in the back of the truck with the pigs. Then the truck set off, bowling along merrily towards Labis.

Throughout the journey the driver chattered and laughed. He was obviously telling me funny stories and making up for my lack of appreciation by applauding himself. And he liked beards, making a point of grasping his wispy example and then pointing to my stubbly one, nodding in approval as he did so. He was so obviously delighted by it and so polite in letting me know that I managed to conceal my fear of a crash as the lorry careered ahead without the benefit of his guiding hands on the steering wheel.

Against all the odds we arrived in Labis safely and I rewarded the truck driver for effort and humour if for nothing else, presenting him with a Calvert chitty. I wrote it out neatly on a page from my notebook. 'On the instructions of Colonel Michael Calvert. Pay the bearer of this note, who has rendered service, the sum of $20.' The driver was impressed. He looked at it for a while then folded it neatly and put it in his breast pocket. Then he looked at me and I held my hand out to him. We shook hands and for the first time since we had met his face was serious. It was as if I had conferred honour on him. In a way I had. I had given him a Calvert chitty.

The chitty was just a piece of paper without purchasing value yet if presented for payment, Calvert, though unaware of my practice of issuing them, would honour it. He would do so because of his awareness of the importance of doing so. A British soldier had issued a promissory note in his name and he could not do otherwise. But the recipients did not see them as a promise of payment though the dollar sign was always plain in the script. They saw them as a tangible sign of recognition for services rendered, a courtesy. The truck driver saw it like that, aware of notice and good form. He had come out of our brief meeting not just having saved face but having enhanced it. That made him very happy.

The chitties were a useful device in all sorts of situations and in the past had settled differences that otherwise would have led to bloody confrontation in the seamier districts of Kuala Lumpur and Singapore. The fact that none had ever been presented for payment said a lot about the significance placed on them by the holders. They were talismans, creators of good will and friendship, of much greater value than the sums they represented.

On our way to the holding camp I kept plenty of room between myself and my companions. During the journey into town they had been careless enough to doze off in the back of the truck with the inevitable result. Now they were badly in need of a hosing down and a liberal dosing of scent.

Pete Kerry and Corporal Dillon met us at the camp gates and looked at us for some time without speaking. Eventually they asked us if we were alright, their tone expressing doubt. They obviously did not believe the evidence of their own eyes. That was understandable when Kerry added that everyone thought we were dead. It seemed that shortly after leaving the troop shots had been heard from the direction we'd taken and it had been assumed that we had made contact with our quarry. Dover waited for our return and when we did not, assumed that we had come off second best in the skirmish. That explained his non-appearance at the RV arranged for the following day. He would not be meeting us at Labis either, having been evacuated to hospital. Another man fallen foul of Malaya's many diseases.

Senior officers of the regiment.

After a meal in the cookhouse I reported for de-briefing. The de-briefing team included a special branch man, two uniformed policemen and an officer of the Regiment. I retraced our movements for them from the moment we had left 18 Troop right up to the time of our arrival in Labis. Hardly any questions were asked and I got the distinct feeling that they were just filling in time, going through the motions. It was all over in an hour. The lads in the cookhouse had made a better job of it.

That night I went out on the town with Mick Dillon. I'd had a good clean up beforehand but left my stubbly beard alone. In time it would grow into one of the finest in the Regiment though by then they were going out of fashion. Calvert encouraged beards; they saved water wasted in the process of shaving. They also fostered confidence and individuality and gave the appearance of toughness and ferocity to the most angelic face. And if men looked tough and fierce they gradually became so. I agreed with that up to a point but could not accept that there were men in the Regiment with a need to acquire toughness and ferocity; most already had more than enough of both, with or without beards.

We visited every beer hall in Labis that evening and spent money in every one of them. Later we were joined by Tommy and John. Neither drank so I supposed that they came just to keep an eye on me. As the night went on more men arrived and between us we put away enough beer to float a troopship. We rolled back to camp in the early hours, one supporting another. There a message awaited me from Major Woodhouse. He wanted me back at Clapham. I kept the news from my companions, time enough to tell them in the morning. I woke them an hour or so after they had gone to sleep and gave them the glad tidings. It was 5.15am. They seemed quite happy about it until I explained that it was here and now, not tomorrow.

We left Labis at 6.00am and along the way flagged down a police jeep. Half an hour later we were at our entry point and soon afterwards in the forest. The going was about the same as it had been some weeks earlier when the Squadron had taken over twelve hours to reach Clapham. We went easy and did it in less than nine, homing in on the camp like racing pigeons.

After his urgent message I had thought that Woodhouse would have wanted a long pow-wow about the value of three-man patrols and the nutritional value of freshly killed pork but after the exchange of a few words he ended our chat. During it I had let him know of our departure time from Labis that morning and the time of our arrival at Clapham. Perhaps he had gone away to compare our time for the journey with his.

The next day was free of patrols and I wondered why I had been ordered back – the Squadron was to go out on the following day anyway and in that context the order did not make much sense. Perhaps it was thought that I'd get up to some mischief if left in the town. In any event the free time was very welcome and I made use of it to get another spot of fishing in.

From the bank of the river it was possible to see the fish and for them to see me. In England that would mean a wasted day for the fisherman and a peaceful one for

Trooper Gregory Lammin in uniform.

the fish. But things are not the same in the jungle as they are in England. On the Wye or the Test the fish are wary of men in hairy suits holding long poles offering succulent morsels attached to a hook. In the jungle stream they are not wary and I caught five in quick time. Then I called it a day. It had been worth coming back just for the fishing.

What remained of D Squadron marched away from Clapham on 21 September 1951. The march went without incident and we arrived at the road eleven hours after starting out. Those still with us could be said to be, using Calvert's words, both tough and ferocious, though fewer than half of them had beards of any note. Still the lack was not a good reason for picking a quarrel with any of them.

Trucks awaited us at the road causing general amazement. Had a revolution taken place in the motor pool? We arrived in Labis without a breakdown. It wasn't a revolution after all but a miracle. At the camp we settled down for the night. There was no alternative; no one in the Squadron had a brass farthing, having spent all they held when joining us two nights previously on our tour of the beer halls. Everyone was resigned to an early night when Woodhouse sprung a surprise. He had laid on beer and skittles in a go down close to the camp and we were all invited. Suddenly Woodhouse was the most popular man in the Regiment.

The interior of the go down was inviting, a baronial hall, tables running its full length, crowded with bottles of Tiger and Carlsberg with reserves stacked against the walls, crate on crate, enough to paralyse every man in the Squadron. The party began in a minor key with quiet storytelling, then as the beer took effect it became louder until we were all shouting jovially over each other. By 10.00pm those who had been foolish enough to listen were suffering from shell-shock, overcome by the tales of general mayhem in the pursuit of war and the reserves still stood against the walls, untouched.

The sing-sing was the highlight of the middle stage of the proceedings. Everyone took part, although some of the contestants sounded like love-lorn tom cats. The sentimentalists, boys standing on the burning deck variety were almost as bad if in a different way, crying when coming to the more poignant lines. When my turn came all the songs and verses known to me had already been heard; I was at a loss and asked to pass. But the master of ceremonies would have none of it. I jumped up on the table and offered to fight anyone in the room or all of them at once if required. That would be my turn. That was fine, meeting with general approval and the rush of takers collapsed the table depositing all in a tangle of arms and legs on the floor. After a short melee honour was satisfied and the festivities resumed.

At the end of the competition voting took place for the best turn of the evening and I won by a street. The party continued on a high note but without any further melees, all had mellowed, pickled in beer. The party closed at 2.00am and we rolled away to seek places for the night. It had been a very successful evening and news of our conviviality quickly spread, leading to another invitation. The members of the planters club would be pleased to entertain us on their premises at 8.00pm that evening, dress optional.

We were all there on the hour. Each man was allotted a host and a hostess for the evening and that suited the storytellers. They now had a fresh audience and before downing the first drink were well into their tales. My hosts were a French couple, man and wife. She was a beauty and though there were many beautiful women in the room she stood out like a silver birch in a pine wood. And she had a wonderful voice, like water sprinkling from a fountain. I'd got first prize again.

Her husband was knowledgeable about military matters and as the night went on it came out that he had served with the French Army in Indo-China for a number of years. He spoke about the difficulties of troop transportation there, particularly in the Delta and I agreed that the solution was water transport – as it is in any territory where the means exists. What was the point of rivers if they were not made use of?

We had much in common. They were Bretons, Celtic as I was and that brought questions from Madame.

'You are not English then?'

'No.' My answer prompted the obvious return.

'Then why are you in the English army?' That was an easy one.

'It's not the English army it's the British Army.'

'You are British then?'

'No, I'm Irish.'

'But you are in the British Army. Why is that?'

'It's a tradition with us.'

'You are a mercenary then?'

'No. I do get paid but hardly enough to buy a plate of shark fin soup.'

'Oh, you like shark fin soup?'

'Well, I don't know, I've never had any.'

F.G. 'Paddy' Boylan.   'Paddy' Boylan's grave.

'Would you like some? Come for supper. You can try it, see if you do like it.' Her husband repeated the invitation and I accepted.

The soup was a disappointment, a poor also ran to mulligatawny. Maybe a pinch or two of curry powder had been missed out in the preparation. That night I slept in a bed that was fit for the Pea Princess. It made up for the soup. After breakfasting with my hosts I returned to camp. Bad news awaited me.

During the night Paddy Boylan had been shot in the chest. He had died at 6.00am, about the time I was dawdling over breakfast. It is hard when a comrade dies but harder when he is also a friend. He had been that and more, a companion in hardship, always ready to spit in the eye of fortune to benefit another, I wanted to cry salt tears for my loss but could not, denied their consolation. It was hard to believe that I would never see him or hear his soft southern brogue ever again. In a short space of time I had gained two new friends and lost an old one. On balance it could be said that I was one up, but I was not.

12

DUEL IN THE SHADE

Three days after leaving Clapham an issue of clothing was made to us. It was needed as we were in rags and our boots were falling to pieces. It made a difference, the men who had previously resembled scarecrows now looked like coat-hangers, thin, but smartly so.

The operation continued that night, the Squadron, now reinforced, marching out just before midnight. There was no moon and a lot of bumping took place causing falls and minor injuries. We moved at less than a mile an hour, making a song and dance about it, doing away with secrecy. It was pointless but went on.

At 3.00am we walked into a lightning storm. An hour later a great wind came up, dashing the rain into our races, striking like a whip. Heads lowered against it causing more stumbling. We were in a melee with a typhoon and it was winning. The lightning ran alongside the column, white hot rods, inches away from us and the ground. When it passed the thunder erupted, ear-splitting, shaking the earth, a giant HE shell exploding less than a foot away, echoing until the next bolt sped by.

We went on, putting one foot in front of the other, churning the ground into mud. Eventually we lay down by the side of the track and waited for the end of the storm and the night. We lay but could not sleep or rest, the cold was arctic. We were numb and aching at the same time, every part hurting like an old wound in winter.

Dawn came after a darkness that had seemed endless and the sun took up the spent rain in grey and white vapours spiralling through the trees like incense from an altar. An hour after sunrise we were in the middle of a vast open air Turkish bath. It warmed us, taking the stiffness out of our limbs. I looked around me, at the men and the new clothing they had paraded so proudly twelve hours before. It now hung limply from their thin frames, bedraggled, covered in mud.

In spite of the rain our rations were dry and we breakfasted. The bergen is an awkward, poorly designed excuse for a pack though fine as a correctional device for round shoulders. It is also waterproof. It had to be useful in one way or another.

We went through strange territory that day, few trees but plenty of sharp spiky grass with edges that cut like razors. At the beginning of the day the open area in which it grew had been welcomed as a change from the twilight of the forest, allowing the sun to warm and dry us. Now, some hours into the march, the sun burned our white faces. By noon every canteen was empty and water, though the storm had ended only six hours earlier, could not be found anywhere. We camped that night with dry canteens, too parched to eat.

At sunset I spread my poncho in a hollow to condense water from the air. At dawn the poncho held less than a pint, a disappointment. On the hills that amount could be gathered in an hour. I split it amongst my section and then took them out to look for a better source of supply and found it; a deep pool hidden in undergrowth, protected from the sun by bowing foliage. We had been led to it by birds. Ounce for ounce they need five times more water than a man and after a thirsty twelve hours of darkness their first need at the dawn is water. All we had to do was watch at first light and then follow them. The water in the pool was cool and clear, but it was stagnant and would have to be boiled before drinking. Such pools were often visited by rats, and the bacteria in rat droppings could cause Weil's disease, otherwise known as Leptospirosis. That was a prospect that most could not bear to think about. There was no cure for it, death was certain, a long and agonising process. Rat catcher's yellow was always lurking, killing those thirsty enough to forget about it. In a land of water it is paradoxical that thirst was always with us, climbing through clouds, soaked outside, dry inside. In the valleys there was an abundance but most of it was still and dangerously polluted. We were told that Mepachrin tablets made it safe but no one believed that. If there was no cure for Weil's disease how could a tablet destroy the cause of it?

We patrolled the dry area for some days, starting early and finishing late. Then Woodhouse, satisfied that the area was clear, ordered a move. Nobody was surprised by the time chosen for it, 2.00am. There was now an obsession with night marches and I accepted the blame for that, as they had only begun after my successful

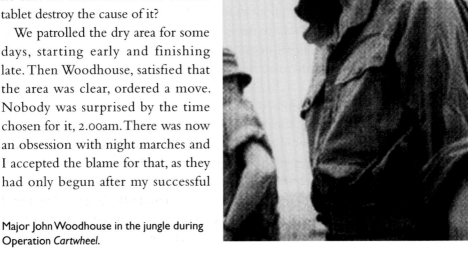

Major John Woodhouse in the jungle during Operation *Cartwheel*.

night trip from Hill 615. The fact that I had travelled light and alone was not taken into account when considering the problem of moving a Squadron in the dark. Or maybe on this occasion it was. An order was given that compasses were to be slung over the backs of every man, the glow from the luminous dial hopefully acting as a lighthouse. A good idea in theory but not in practice.

The start of the march was a taste of things to come, the compasses jumping around on our backs like hyperactive fleas. Sometimes the dials could be seen but most times they could not and bumping was once again the order of the night. The leading scout added to the confusion, stopping and starting at irregular moments for no apparent reason. When he halted the Squadron closed up like a concertina resulting in falls and curses. Our initial destination was a road no more than two miles from the start line, partly through the forest but mainly through a rubber estate, an easy hour's stroll in the light. But we were in the dark, stumbling around like the blinded Cyclops, and it took three hours.

Once on the road we moved north for an hour and then re-entered the forest on the eastern side, going on until noon. During the midday halt our tiredness caused tempers to fray and there were heated arguments. Troopers Trela and Conway came close to blows. That was only avoided when I got between them and read them the riot act. Both piped down and I sent Conway to the rear. The further away he was from Trela the better it would be for all concerned.

Things had barely settled down when Major Woodhouse left the head of the column and came back along the track. He had sensed that something was wrong. When sure that all was in order he nodded, turned and went back. But things were not in order. Trela and Conway had not been on good terms for some time. The ill feeling between them had started soon after the evacuation of Corporal Dover, but I hadn't been there at the time and didn't know the reason for it. I didn't want to know. It was enough that the matter simmered on, interfering with the efficiency of the troop.

That evening the Squadron set up a semi-permanent base camp, and early next morning the first patrol went out, the honour going to 18 Troop. Sergeant Smithers now commanded. He had joined us at Labis, Woodhouse having appointed me after the loss of Corporal Dover. From the beginning of the patrol I was impressed by him. He set a sensible pace and at halts positioned sentries at the front and rear of the column, hidden at the side of the track. It was not the perfect way but as close to it as I had seen in the past few weeks. He was, it seemed, more than a set of balanced stripes.

Two hours into the patrol, just after the leading scout had crossed a small stream, the accident happened. Sergeant Smithers was the next to cross but fell, one leg caught up in a tangle of tree roots, his upper body falling forward into the water. Fortunately it was shallow and he was in no danger of drowning, but when we got to him he was in great pain, the tendons in his trapped leg damaged, possibly severed. But he made little of it, refusing morphine. After freeing him we carried him to the bank and removed his boot. The injury was severe, his ankle swollen to twice its normal size, either broken or dislocated with additional injury to the Achilles tendon. There was no question of him going on and that posed a problem. Should we return to base or carry on with the patrol? I gave that some thought. If Smithers had died in the river I would have gone on, it was the duty of the troop, so I decided that the patrol had to continue. Smithers agreed. He needed rest before beginning the trek back to base anyway, it was the best medicine. We left him in a safe place with Cambell and McDonald to keep him company and attend to any emergency that might arise.

When satisfied that he was settled in we continued the patrol, crossing the stream and going on beyond it. All was quiet and at noon we halted for the midday break. Less than five minutes later Trela and Conway resurrected their quarrel. On the march they had been at opposite ends of the column, and at the halt, when moving off the track, I had made sure that they did so with plenty of space between them, but obviously to no avail. They had made a bee-line for each other as soon as they were in the trees. The matter was getting serious and had to be brought to an end.

When I caught up to them blows had already been exchanged, both men marked about the face, Conway to a greater extent than Trela. He had obviously got the worst of it and now held his rifle with the muzzle pointed at Trela's midriff, safety catch off, taunting him to come on. Trela would do that and fairly soon; he was looking for a weak spot but from where I stood there wasn't one, the rifle cocked, first pressure on the trigger applied. Soon there would be one corpse, possibly two. Trela would not die immediately even with a .303 in his gut, and in the intervening period he would close and probably break Conway's neck. It was not a prospect to relish and a difficult one to explain to Woodhouse. He would put it all down to me, say that I had allowed it to get out of hand.

I looked for an opportunity and when Trela moved back a step I got between them. He was now safe for the moment unless Conway decided to shoot both of us. Just in case he did I grabbed the barrel of his rifle and pushed it off target, keeping a firm hold so that it could not be re-aligned. Check, but for how long? There was no doubt that the argument had reached a point where drastic action was needed to resolve it.

A fist fight was out of the question, both were already injured and if they fought they would end up badly hurt. Isolation had been tried and had failed and in any case both were now in a cold rage, ready to use weapons. Distance would not count for much in that situation. There was only one solution and the difficulty would be to persuade them to accept it: a training-style Scout duel, the manhunt and the aimed shot. It would be deadly if they accepted and then ignored the rules but if the worst came to the worst it would mean the death of only one of them instead of two. Now I had to get them to agree to take part in the game. I was still between them and it was not a position that induced quick thought, half of my mind concentrated on the effort of keeping hold of Conway's rifle and the other half on what would happen if the hold was broken. Eventually I decided to play on their pride, question their courage. That would direct anger my way lessening it between them, making them receptive to the idea.

From the beginning of the confrontation the tableau under the trees had remained as if frozen in time, everyone silent, watching and waiting to see if I could get the better of the situation. Now I looked at them and thought, should I order them to intervene? It was a tempting idea but I rejected it. There was no purpose in ordering an action that could turn into a general melee. Instead I spoke to Trela and Conway.

'Neither of you ever took part in the hunts at Dusun Tua did you?' I knew they had but why concede that if the purpose was to make them appear less than they were? The question startled them. 'Are either of you game enough to have a go at it now?' They said nothing, the silence oppressive, and I grew nervous, my knuckles white from the effort of keeping Conway's rifle out of harm's way. In the end they accepted the challenge and I qualified the rules. 'No unlimited time, if you can't get a shot off within ten minutes that will count as the end of it.' Enough time had already been wasted and I was getting impatient. They were aware of that, nodded and went into the forest.

The minutes ticked away and I began to have doubts. They were both their own man and from pride alone may well have made variations to the agreement. Nine minutes passed and I began to count the seconds of the tenth. There were ten to go when a shot rang out. They came out of the: trees together and I looked at their faces. It was settled and I went to them and let them choose places in the column. They chose to stay together.

It was now too late to patrol any further and we turned around and headed back to base, picking up Sergeant Smithers and his guard on the way. All three were in good form; the rest had done them good. The Sergeant's injuries had also improved and after tight bandaging he was able to get about, if slowly. He asked about the patrol and I reported all well, though it was better than that. We made slow time on the way back. Smithers did his best but even with two men to help him he was unable to keep up any pace. Soon after our arrival Major Woodhouse asked for a word. On reporting he expressed concern about Smithers and then said that an ambush party was going out that night and would I like to join it? It wasn't a question and I was not over the moon about the invite but gave the expected reply.

We set off just before sunset, Woodhouse leading. The light went soon afterwards and we were immediately stumbling over the uneven ground, making alien noises easily heard by those whose very lives depended on hearing. There are better times to travel. We were in position at 7.30pm. The ambush was sprung three hours later when shots were fired, a bloody business. We remained in position until 5.20am.

Later that morning there was yet another re-organisation of the Squadron, the three remaining troops reduced to two. We had got replacements at Labis and I didn't see the need for it. Squadron strength was down to 40 but that in my view was still enough to keep not just three troops but all four. It was not the time to draw in our horns, dispensing with the cohesion and loyalties of small groups, but rather a time to reinforce them, make them more with less, the few, the happy band of brothers. The shock came with the announcement that the troop to be disbanded was my own, 18. It was hard to believe, the best of all to go, why? It had no commander but it had always functioned well without one. We had had five in the past month but 18 Troop had remained. No longer. We were going the way of 17 Troop.

Sergeant Smithers was evacuated on 28 September. We took him to the road, killing two birds with one stone, as a re-supply truck was expected. We started early but his injury kept the pace down and the journey took almost three hours. He was in constant pain throughout but apart from one instance when he stumbled, taking a nasty fall, there was not a sound of complaint from him. Another minor miracle awaited us at the road; the trucks were already there.

While they were being unloaded I kept Smithers company. It didn't take long and when completed I helped him on to the 15 cwt. I was sorry to see him go. He knew his job and was easy to get on with. The accident had been unfortunate in more ways than one. If it had not happened there would have been no excuse to disband 18 Troop.

We got the supplies back to base later that afternoon, each man humping over 90 pounds plus arms and ammunition. They were distributed on the following morning and we breakfasted. Afterwards the camp was struck and we set off for a new area. The first part of the trek retraced our steps of the previous day and when that became apparent there was a fair amount of mumbled cursing from those who had acted as pack mules fourteen hours before. Why hadn't the supplies been left under guard at the drop off point for dishing out now rather than a few hours previously? It would have saved a lot of back breaking work. As it was they had been carried in and now they had been carried out again to the self same place.

After leaving the forest that morning we went on to a rubber estate. It was a pleasant place to be with nothing to impede our way, the trees spaced, giving views in all directions. Between the branches gaps allowed sunlight to enter, dappling the ground giving it the appearance of rippling water. The rubber tappers, mainly Tamil women, were at work cutting chevron-shaped grooves in the tree trunks, encouraging the latex to flow. It dripped into small cup-like containers which, though seeming to fill slowly, were always full when the tapper finished cutting and returned to the starting point to empty them into a bucket.

We were on the Pogah estate and the men made play with the name when near the women, stopping in front of them, pointing to the ground and saying 'Pogah' in an enquiring way. The women, assuming that they were being asked to confirm the name of the estate, smiled and nodded their heads vigorously. Their response caused a lot of amusement. We laughed at their innocent misinterpretation and pronunciation of the word and they laughed because we did.

After crossing the estate we went back into the forest and close to sunset made camp. At dawn on the following morning we set off to march the perimeter of the estate. We kept close to the edge of the forest, the dark background of the trees hiding us from the sight of anyone in the rubber. The view of the trees in the early morning, before the tappers are at work, has the appearance of a cathedral, the tree trunks pillars, supporting a high arched roof of leaves, filtering and colouring light as efficiently as stained glass.

The circuit of the estate took nine hours. There was no activity. During the following three days the exercise was repeated. The only return was knowledge of the tappers as individuals, the ability to greet them by name. They were a gentle, civilised people with a positive outlook on life. Their day like ours began early, they were at work soon after dawn – the latex flows best then. Their early start was compensated by an early finish. At noon they drifted away from the trees and went to have the morning's harvest measured. Then they went home to prepare their midday meal. By 1.00pm the estate was deserted and a calm set in amongst the trees, an uninhabited world. We walked around it, goldfish on the outside of the bowl.

13

EMPEROR KANG AND BAD NEWS

Kang was possibly the most popular man in D Squadron. He was our Chinese liaison officer, confidant of Calvert and a man of parts. He spoke English with a plum in his mouth, Malay like a Sultan and any number of Chinese dialects. Shooting and tracking were second nature to him, he was tireless on the march and ate less than Woodhouse – who could go a day or two on a handful of peanuts.

I was on road watch with him on 2 October 1951; not so much a duty as an exclusive interview with a sage. Like all the Chinese he had a well developed sense of humour. More importantly he laughed when I told him a droll tale, while others waited for the punch line that had already been delivered.

We were waiting to contact the supply truck which was a day overdue. It was such a regular occurrence that I often wondered why it was never allowed for. Why not request supplies one or two days before they were actually required? Or better still sort the quartermaster and the O/C motor pool out, teach them the difference between one and two.

While we waited, hidden in the brush alongside the road, Kang told stories. He was a fund of them, the best concerning his descent from the Chinese emperor Kangxi. It was an excellent tale that I had heard many times before and did not mind hearing again. He told it in a way unlike all the others, defensive and strident at the same time, wanting to be believed and willing to do something about it if he was not. As far as I was concerned everyone was descended from somebody so why not a Chinese emperor? After all, the landed gentry of England and most members of the House of Lords seemed to be descended from the mistresses of Charles II. Kangxi had lived 30 generations ago so by now there must be thousands of his descendants floating about. It would have been difficult in the circumstances to exclude Kang from that numerous band.

When he finished the tale I applauded as required, and he asked me about my ancestry. He thought I would not know and that would enhance his; but if the frog would cause all sensible people to play possum for the rest of the night, so one way or another we were wasting our time. We were in place by 7.00pm and lay out for almost twelve hours without result, quitting at 6.20am. When we arrived back at the base the events of the night were made clear. A party of insurgents had passed through our ambush position half an hour before we arrived. They had been engaged later by a number of auxiliaries with the usual result. Still they had been in the right place at the right time. Moving to a position in the dark is counter-productive, far better to move in the light, hidden by the forest, lying up near the position and travelling the last few yards in darkness.

Later that morning, Saturday 6 October, the 1/2 Gurkhas laid down a mortar bar-rage on the swamp into which the guerrillas had escaped. They worked with a will, raining down hundreds of bombs into the mud, ceasing fire at 11.00am. The bombard-ment had gone on for two and a half hours. We entered the swamp at 11.05am and cleared it by 2.30pm. Afterwards, back at the base, Woodhouse collared me again. He passed the time of day pleasantly enough and that should have warned me that he had something serious to say as a follow up. He had. I was given a direct order to proceed out that afternoon and prepare for the signaller course. He was making a lot out of a little but if I refused to obey the order it would mean a certain court-martial. It was Hobson's choice. I went out later that day in the company of Sergeant Sutherland, 'Robin Hood', 'Black Jake' and the last remaining members of my old section in 18 Troop, Mousey and Snakeribs. Robin Hood had been named for his skill in obtaining food and drink, whatever the circumstances. I had tried for a long time to draft him into my section but without success, loyalty being another of his qualities.

Sergeant Hanna met us at the road, sitting in a 15-cwt truck. I was surprised when he said that we were not going into Labis but to Dusun Tua. So much for the rumour that we had left there for good. The ride to Selangor was hair-raising; the driver broke every speed limit along the way to Kuala Lumpur and every by-law when he drove through it. He slowed at the entrance to the camp at Dusun Tua and when he stopped outside the guardroom I got off the truck very quickly. He might well decide to do a lap of honour around the billets and I did not want to accompany him on it. He had broken the record for the journey between Johore and Selangor by two hours, travel-ling mainly in the dark. That was sufficient for the day as far as I was concerned.

It was close to midnight when we arrived and I entered the guardroom in the hope that there would be some tea going and was met by Pete Kerry. He had watched my hurried descent from the truck and was still smiling about it. We sat down together and chatted. The Regiment now had a fast growing constabulary, he being a founder member. In spite of that he didn't take the job too seriously, though dressing the part. His webbing shone, black as coal, the brasses burnished to gold, the creases in his shirt and shorts dangerous to the touch. He looked well though his face showed most of his fourteen years of service, all in crab stations. I was pleased to see him and more so when he admitted to solvency, a happy situation arising out of the fact that all the card sharps had been otherwise engaged in the past month. Card playing was his delight

The author and Pete Kerry at ease in the mess hall.

and during his service he had lost enough money at it to buy himself out and have enough left to set up in Civvy Street. Not that he would consider such an action; he was part and parcel of the army and would never leave it voluntarily. Still I was pleased that he had not been able to indulge his fancy for some time. There were better things to spend money on and on the following night it was spent on beer. When the last dollar was gone we returned to camp fairly upright and turned in.

My bunk was comfortable and I had supped a lot of beer but in spite of that I was unable to sleep. As was usual in such situations I made use of the time to think, going over the events of the past few days. The re-training issue was known about in the camp and had already caused a lot of discontent, some of it expressed forcibly earlier that evening. It also caused me to consider my position very closely. If re-training was on the agenda why was I being shunted off on a signals course while it took place? Why was it thought that I, unlike all the others, was not in need of it? After thinking about it for some time I concluded that as a leading member of the awkward squad I was being nudged gently aside. I had been chosen to twiddle with the knobs of wireless sets while a critical period in the life of the Regiment was about to begin. Changes would be made while I was elsewhere; but one way or another I intended to circumvent them.

The High Commissioner, Sir Henry Gurney, was killed on 6 October. We were clearing swamp land after the Gurkha bombardment at the time. The convoy in which he was travelling was ambushed at the Gap, Fraser Hill. It was a classic guerrilla attack taking place when the vehicles had slowed to negotiate a sharp bend in the road. In spite of a speedy follow up the attackers retired without loss. We would brush with them later.

palms to heaven, smile and go away hoping for better things in the following week. He never pressed for payment though all of his extended family in far away India depended on him for their every need. In many instances he faced the same dangers as his debtors but without their compensations. If he died on the battlefield there would be no pension for his wife or his children. If he was crippled or blinded he would go from honourable trade to hopeless beggary.

I had been a good customer of the train cha-wallah, drinking a lot of tea and paying for every drop and when the train pulled into the station at Johore Bahru I dropped him an extra dollar. It would pay for some of the cha he hadn't been paid for in the past.

The journey had taken ten and a half hours and I still had to get to the school which was about seven miles away. There was a bus service of sorts but I had no money left and looked for other means of transport. About an hour later I found it, a truck driven by a Gurkha – they seem to pop up everywhere. We arrived at the school in the dark. It was a big place judging by the lights shining from hundreds of windows, as big as the School of Infantry in Wiltshire. The Gurkha reported in at the guardroom, S and PD, and a provost pointed me in the direction of the signallers' quarters.

The camp buildings were of timber, lit by electricity, the barrack rooms luxurious, furnished with fine wire mesh beds, a chair by each one – the commissariat had obviously gone mad. There was one vacant bunk in the signallers' basha and I stowed my gear under it and turned in. The other occupants were asleep and I was pleased to hear that the snorers were all grouped together at the far end of the room. We obviously had a guiding hand amongst us.

Almost as soon as I got my head down I fell asleep and woke almost immediately, or so I thought. In fact it was 2.00am and bells and drums were echoing around the camp. We were under attack and I dressed quickly and grabbed my rifle. Below the barrack room on a square of flat ground about 100 figures were milling around. They were

Relaxing outside a basha.

not attacking but were continuing the row that had convinced me that they were, and at 2.00am one is as bad as the other. I went down the hill to find out what it was all about and on arrival saw that they were Gurkhas, all in a state of drunkenness. I walked through them to the middle of the square and held my hand up to get their attention. If the row was not stopped the whole camp would soon be awake.

There was plenty of light for them to see me, lamp standards dotted the area, but they pretended I wasn't there and went on with their frolics. After a while, my arm got so stiff that I decided to get their attention by other means. I shouted, a good RSM's bellow, louder than the bells and drums combined. When the echoes died away, one of the group, a naik, came to me with his hand out and spoke. 'Christmas, Christmas.' He was not only drunk but two and a half months out with his calendar reading as well: it was 12 October. He was obviously too far gone to reason with so I ignored his hand and told him to get everybody off to bed. But he took no notice and kept repeating the words.

When he stopped for breath, I told him in words and signs that he and his friends had to leave. I indicated his friends and then pointed to an area of the camp that would take all of them well away from my billet. While doing this he stumbled into me and I held him up; he would have fallen to the ground otherwise. As I held him his friends closed in around us, one coming so close that I had to push him back. It wasn't a hard push but he stumbled and fell and when he got up he had a knife in his hand. I kept my ground, waiting for the thrust, but it didn't come. The knife had been produced as a reflex action and when the Gurkha was back on his feet he returned it to the scabbard – which was just as well. I'd have shot him if he had attempted to strike and then possibly I'd have had to shoot his friends as well. The naik had disappeared but now reappeared and offered me a drink. It was a small cup, wine possibly or maybe rum. I didn't find out because I refused it. Yet the reason for refusal was gone, the drums and bells now silent and the men drifting away. Suddenly I began to regret that I was such a light sleeper and that I had refused the drink offered by the Corporal.

As I moved away from the scene I saw a figure in the shadows just out of reach of the cones of light from the lamps. As I came closer the figure moved and a voice asked if I was alright. The accent was familiar and reassuring and I replied that I was. As I continued up the hill he fell in beside me and we walked side by side to the barrack room. He was also on the signals course and had the bunk next to mine.

He was a marine, a member of 42 Commando and a fellow Celt, Pat Gallagher; references enough for anybody. I asked him why he had followed me out of the barrack room.

'I didn't follow you in the first place. I went out to see what was going on and when I saw you going into that lot, I thought they're might be trouble so I followed on. You might have needed a bit of help.'

That was true. He was carrying a sten gun and I was curious about what he would have done if real trouble had started. I pointed to it.

'What would you have done with that?'

'I would have used it.' I was sure he would but wondered how. 'Would you have killed?'

'No, that wouldn't be needed, a burst over their heads would have been enough.'

'What if it wasn't?'

'Then a few around their toes.'

'But what if that didn't work?'

'Oh, it would.' He seemed confident about that.

'OK, you've done all that and they're still coming on getting close and they're very angry. What now?'

'I'd shorten their legs a bit.' He spoke in a matter of fact way, his soft southern accent creating a picture in my mind of him doing just that – and changing magazines when required with the cool of a firearms instructor at target practice. But was he cool or deadly cold? He must have guessed what I was thinking and after what seemed a long time he spoke again. 'You must know what I would have done or you wouldn't keep on asking the same question using different words. If my life is in the balance I am entitled to protect it in the best way I can. The best way would be to kill those who want to kill me but they were only armed with knives so there wasn't a need for that. Legs are repairable, corpses aren't.'

Next day there was gossip in the camp about the early morning incident but it went no further than that. The Gurkhas laughed it off, it was just a misunderstanding. And

Getting back to nature on the signals course.

that one word summed it all up as far as I was concerned. I had misunderstood, and almost created a bloody situation in the process.

When the Gurkha told me it was Christmas he meant to convey the information that it was one of their most significant holy days; I must have been half asleep not to understand what he meant and had barged in without giving it any thought. Now all I could do was regret it. It was not the perfect way to start a new venture but one positive thing had come out of it. I had met a soldier with all the qualities a soldier should have, learning a great deal in my first few hours back at school.

The signals course class was a mixed bag, Highlanders, Lowlanders, Manchester's, Royal West Kent's and the Royal Marine Pat Gallagher. I wondered how naval personnel managed to get into an army school. I meant to ask but never got round to it.

The senior instructor on the course was Sergeant Tattersall, aided by Sergeant O'Brien. Both were good soldiers and excellent teachers; better than any I had come across in my schooldays. That was evident before the end of the first day. Both spoke on matters that I was already aware of; I could have related the details of the subjects backwards. That being so I should have been bored but wasn't. The lessons were presented so well and put across so ably that I gave them my full attention. Anybody who wants to learn should be allowed to study under army instructors. They are the best.

On 17 October I got news from my ex-regiment in Egypt, letters from Joe Madden and Tommy Duffy. My old company had just come through a bloody confrontation with paramilitary police in Ishmalia. (Though the troubles began in October the storming of the police barracks took place on 25 January 1952.) The trouble had been brewing for a long time and had turned to armed conflict when the police killed a number of unarmed soldiers. They had then seized the offices of the Suez Canal Company and other properties belonging to foreign nationals. It was as good as a declaration of war and for once the troops were not just allowed, but ordered to strike back. The Lancashire Fusiliers and particularly C Company bore the brunt of the fighting that followed and were honoured to do so.

After some days of street-fighting the police, 700 strong, were driven back and took up defensive positions in the fortified barracks close to the Sweetwater Canal. They held out for two days; C Company then breached the defences and entered the barracks. Once inside they quickly disposed of the matter, the police having split into ten-man units, each unit defending small rooms in the building. It was a curious way to use a large force and the price was duly paid. Prisoners were taken and some of my friends were killed. One of them, Bunny Allen, was hit going over the perimeter wall in the final assault and died shortly after the end of the action. Two brothers, Jim and Harold Eastham, were also killed. That would be hard for the family to take, two sons going within an hour of each other. It would also be hard for the parents of Nick Lowe. He had left England just three weeks before and had been with the Regiment for only eighteen days when he was killed.

Bunny Allen had not been long out of boy service when he died. He had shown great promise as a soldier and was a fine welterweight boxer. I looked at the words

The author relaxing at Nuffield Pool in Singapore, 1952.

A view of Singapore harbour.

about him in Madden's letter and could see his lanky frame again and the smile that never left his face. His family lived in Preston and I thought of writing but then saw it as an intrusion. The company commander would do that anyway and better than I could. Instead I wrote to Major T.P. Shaw OIC and Major Woodcock OC C Company. T.P. had lost a prospect and Major Woodcock some of his best men.

At the end of the first week of the course we were paid and all the scholars headed for Singapore. I went there with Gallagher. I'd arranged to meet friends from the Regiment and it was an opportunity for him to meet them at the same time. He was the sort to fit in with their way of thinking and doing things and I had no doubt that they would get along very well. The meet was at the Union Jack Club in the city centre and when we arrived there were fifteen or so men from A and D Squadrons already there. We joined them and I introduced Gallagher. He hit if off with them right from the start.

All the squadrons were now in Singapore, billeted in barracks outside the city and our reasons for being there were still being invented. The newest was that we had been pulled out to be re-equipped – even though there was no sign of new equipment. What were we to be equipped with? McDonald suggested ray guns and water-wings.

One thing was not in doubt. The move, whatever the reason given, was not acceptable to the majority of the men and resentment against it was growing. We talked about that for a long time. The result was the formation of an ad hoc committee. It was not a revolutionary act but a means of channelling opposition to a prolonged stay on the island. After the meeting we went to the barracks where I was surprised to meet Corporal Dover. The last time I'd seen him was outside Labis when I'd left him to go after the insurgent. I'd thought that he was still in hospital but he quite obviously was not, looking hale and hearty, and I congratulated him on his recovery.

By the time the Regiment had been on the island over a fortnight many of the men were fed up with the humdrum of barrack life. We felt marooned. After breakfasting one morning I returned to quarters with Gallagher. It was his first visit to a regimental barracks and he had been asking questions since his arrival, I was hoarse answering them. On entering the barrack room I saw an apparition, old Mick O'Brien. I'd thought he'd been invalided out and looking at him that seemed to have been an opportunity missed. He was grey in the face and drawn, listless and slow moving. His hand shook when he held it out and was clammily cold. He was a shadow of what he had been only a few months before, but worse, seemed to have lost heart. He mentioned his evacuation on the march out from Clapham, apologising for what was no more than human frailty. I'd never heard him speaking in such a defeatist way before, completely out of character but in keeping with his present mood and obvious ill health. He was drained of hope and that was hard to accept. The stay in hospital had obviously depressed him, it was plain in his whole attitude but the soldier was still there, somewhere inside, obviously from his immaculate turnout, a guardsman from tip to toe. This was all the more remarkable in that it was Sunday, scruff order time. But nothing could disguise the pallor and aged look of his face. He had soldiered too long and it showed.

The trials of inactivity: a round of golf in Singapore.

I tried to josh him into his more usual self.

'Come on Mick, me and Gallagher are going into town. Come with us, it's on me.'

The on me bit should have done the trick; he was as close as Scrooge and would sup with the devil if he was paying. But it didn't work and when the prospect of free ale failed it was hard to think of something that would succeed. 'What about a drink in the canteen then?'

'No, I can't go. I'm too tired.' He was and I changed tack.

'OK then let's sit down for a bit and see how you feel after a rest.' We sat on his bunk and continued to chat. One way or another I was going to put him on the road back to what he had been.

The SAS had been an important part of his life since 1941 and I saw his memories of that time and the succeeding years as factors that would make him whole again. Glories remembered influence the present and he had to be made to remember. It was not easy. We asked questions and he answered them but no more than that. Gallagher geed him on and I jumped in when he ran out of puff. At last we got him off to a hesitant start. He spoke and stopped and we got him going again. He told of the past, Africa, Sicily, Italy, France, Germany and Norway. The more he spoke the better he looked. There was colour in his face and I could see him when he was 25.

He recited a litany of names and places and desperate actions but only dwelt on his matches with Calvert and Mayne. He did not say which of them had broken his nose, though one of them had. Perhaps he spoke with such pride because of his remembrance of those two bouts as well as his love of boxing generally. After our bare-knuckle fight at Dusun Tua he had treated me to a bottle of Tiger, a hitherto unheard of extravagance on his part. Maybe he had seen the bout as a revival of the traditional sport of the Regiment. He was a traditionalist and any return to the past had to be worth a bottle of beer, even if he had to pay for it.

He was soon in full flow giving a blow by blow account of his two most famous matches, relishing every word, enunciating every syllable carefully to be sure that we understood completely. He had come off second best in both contests – 'But I was on my feet at the end.' He said that with the pride of a child and I believed him though it was hard to imagine him giving best while still able to keep his feet. He was on his feet now with spirit in him but still would not come with us and we left him, remembering things past. He would never be fit enough for hard service again but had plenty of it behind him, seventeen years, too much maybe. Pension time was four years away and when leaving I made a fervent wish that he lived to draw it and draw it for as long as he wished.

On the way back to Kota Tinggi with Gallagher later that afternoon I had another surprise meeting. Kang was on the bus. It was the first time I'd seen him since our vigil on the road outside Labis. He looked up as we boarded and waved us to seats next to him. He beamed and I beamed back and it was hard to say which of us was more pleased. Then we settled down to gossip.

The previous few weeks had gone well for him. He had seven weeks' back pay and was going up-country, familiar territory. Would we like to join him? Gladly, if only we could. He understood and made nothing of our refusals. He was going to Kuala Lumpur to visit friends and spend his pay.

'Singapore is too expensive. In KL its two for one, value for money.'

I admired his strength of will. If I wanted something and could pay for it I would want it there and then. We left the bus at Johore Bahru and Kang continued his journey north. I hoped he got his two for one. He deserved such an exchange or better. Two days after his arrival in Kuala Lumpur a platoon of the Royal West Kent Regiment was ambushed outside the town and severely mauled. Again it was the work of Ah Hoi. Kang was not involved in the skirmish but a young soldier from the regiment, a fellow member of the signals course, lost two of his friends in the action and took it very badly. The RWKs, like most regiments, had a lot of national servicemen in the ranks, as high as 60 per cent in some cases. They were keen soldiers but lacked experience and suffered accordingly.

17

THE HAPPY WORD AND THE ROUND ROBIN

Lack of money has been the lot of the soldier since soldiering began. In my case it was chronic, an inconvenience that I'd not managed to come to terms with in spite of many efforts to do so. The problem had arisen soon after my marriage, a union that was to prove the truth of the saying that to marry in haste is to repent at leisure. I had repented a lot since the happy event.

The match had been a harebrained business from the beginning. I'd met the girl while on leave from the army in Egypt. She was a Gypsy and very beautiful and I pursued her from the moment I first set eyes on her. It took a month to persuade her to marry and two days later, my leave up, I returned to the Middle East. The problems, money and otherwise, began then, or maybe when I boarded the troopship *Empire Pride* at Liverpool Docks. In any event, fairly quickly. When I was out of sight she saw herself as a free ace again and went back to the roving life. A year after sailing that was confirmed when I heard that I was the father of twins – a late birth she said, a super-late one I said but to no avail, the paymaster insisting that I was the legal father, docking my pay for the maintenance of the infants. He had already docked it to keep the mother and my share of it was now so small that I wondered why my name was kept on the imprest account. I did everything I could to cancel the payments but without success and they went on and on.

After the birth of the twins she continued along the primrose path and less than a year later I became a father for the third time. I now had five dependents, three children, their mother and her current paramour. She had discarded the twin-getter soon after her first confinement, and though I could not approve the practice of chopping and changing I was relieved that it had been made. If it had not, it was odds on that my dependents would have increased by two instead of one. That was demonstrated if not positively proven by another happy event that occurred about the same time. Her discarded Romeo had taken up with a new love as soon as he was put on the transfer list and after the usual lapse of time she duly presented him with a matching pair. No

The author with his unreliable wife (removed), wearing the beret of the 1st Lancashire Fusiliers, Egypt, 1950.

claim was made against me for the second double top for which I was suitably grateful – paymasters are sentimental folk and if a claim had been made it would have received serious consideration. There were no further claims from my wife in the succeeding months and I presumed that she had taken a vow of celibacy, settling down to a less demanding lifestyle. Hopefully it would continue, as my weekly pay was now down to ten shillings, insufficient to take care of any more of her boyfriends.

Money-wise Mr Micawber epitomised my situation, an income of a pound and an expenditure of a pound and a penny. It was unlikely that I would be jailed for debt, for apart from the taxman my creditors were also my friends, but that did not lessen my embarrassment at being unable to pay my way. However, while unable to make up the shortfall I was able to curb expenditure by avoiding public transport whenever possible. That meant hitching on any transport available, any at least until one particularly memorable journey on a logging truck.

A meeting of the ad hoc committee had been arranged for Saturday 27 October in the UJC Singapore and I had to attend, so I would have to hitch. While getting ready for the trip, Gallagher, also short of funds, offered to keep me company. Private Mott, another would-be signaller and man of means, offered to pay our fares but I turned the offer down diplomatically, saying that hitching was faster than going by bus. Remarkably he believed me and asked if he could join us; speed without cost it seemed, was a combination that even a rich man's son could not resist.

We boarded a logging truck in Johore Bahru. The driver, an amiable Chinese, offered seating in the cab but as there wasn't enough room for three we got in the back, on top of the load. It was not an ideal way to travel; the logs, huge tree trunks bound with chains, moved within their restraints, opening gaps when the truck was in motion, closing without warning with bone-crushing force. We took precautions to avoid the traps, travelling upright, hands whitely held on the chain stanchions, balancing on the logs like lumberjacks on a river run.

On level stretches of the road the movement of the load was regular and predictable, making it easy to maintain balance. That changed when it veered or the camber altered, the logs then taking on a life of their own, moving erratically, snapping like piranhas. I kept clear of the gaps during the early stages of the journey by keeping to one log, going with the rolls, hoping that I was not being guided into one of the many holes opening and closing all around us. When cornering the load moved from one side of the truck to the other, piling up and then falling back to the centre like a wave crashing on a beach. At such times the one-man one-log technique had to be abandoned, a mad frantic scrambling taking its place, hopping from log to log, the only way to avoid entrapment.

By the time we reached the causeway I was expert at remaining upright on objects intent on the opposite and at last had the confidence to look around me. Gallagher and Mott were still in the land of the living and that surprised me. Gallagher no, Mott yes. Yet there he was, bold as brass and appearing to be enjoying himself. By rights his remains should have been sticking to the timber under our feet and I immediately reassessed him. He had been hiding his light under a bushel, a better man than I'd thought.

As we crossed the causeway it began to rain. Up to that point I had believed that as log jumpers we had been tested to the full, but was wrong. The real test was just about to begin. It had been difficult to balance on dry logs but now, greased with water, it became a nightmare of effort for nerves and sinews. We had hopped fairly frequently from the beginning but now had to hop all the time and soon it became harder to lift my feet, almost too hard. But fear is a powerful motivating force and I kept the frantic running on the spot going.

Soon after the rain began we entered a village and the driver slowed to avoid hitting any of the scrawny chickens that darted from one side of the road to the other. The slower speed had no effect on the logs however, the ruts in the road more than compensating for that. They continued to crash from side to side at an alarming rate and we continued to dance a frenzied fandango on top of them. Our performance must have been eye-catching for in spite of the rain it attracted an appreciative audience of villagers. They were entranced, and clapped and cheered like a football crowd.

Progress through the village was slowed further when the kamikaze chickens were joined by numerous children and a pack of dogs, adding tremolo screams and excited barks to the outraged squawks of the poultry. The slower pace was appreciated, enabling those who had missed our entry to the village to catch the continuing performance by sprinting from one end of the street to the other, joining the throng already there. They were easy to please, applauding every movement made, cheering when a particularly intricate tap-dance took place.

For a time I doubted the motive for their appreciation. Were they enthusing over our undoubted skill or pandering to the hope that one, or better still all three of us, would misstep and finish up between the logs? Perhaps they had mistaken us for the advance guard of a travelling circus and were applauding, in all sincerity, acrobats engaged in nothing more than their usual activities? It was easier to control fear while they watched, even act the bravo, allowing me to raise my eyes and look around again. Gallagher was going great guns, moving like a ballet dancer, his feet twinkling like fire

Troopers enjoying a drink in the Union Jack Club.

flies. Would he do well in the Royal Ballet or did he need an element of danger in order to turn in a virtuoso performance? Mott was also doing well, prancing gleefully. Both were doing fine but I was not, but I lacked the courage to bang on the driver's cab and bring the ball to a close.

When we eventually got to Singapore I got off the lorry with trembling legs. The driver gave a knowing smile when I thanked him for the lift. We shook hands and I smiled back at him. It was a definite goodbye; au revoirs are for things you want to revisit, certainly not for a return match with a lorry load of two-ton logs.

My travelling companions, none the worse for their exertions, came with me to the Union Jack Club where I drank their health and they drank mine. They were still there when Matt Trela and others from the Squadron arrived, greeting Gallagher like a long-lost brother. Mott was also quickly on good terms with them, surprising me yet again. It was becoming obvious that my judgment of character was not as good as it used to be.

crimson of cropped combs. Their eyes were fierce and all-seeing, showing eagerness for the bloody work ahead.

The master of the main signalled and the leg straps were removed and the birds stood free on opposite sides of the pit. They watched one another for a moment and then moved with silent savage fury. They went in feet first, high in the air, the higher pounding down, needle-sharp steel spurs tearing an eye from the other, leaving a red hole in its place. It was a disappointment for the spectators. The one eyed cock would now die quickly and those who had bet on him were murderous in his agony. He had cheated them out of their money and the amusement derived from a long gruelling contest, each bird whittling the other away feather by feather, comb, flesh and eyes. Eyes should always be last, plucked out at leisure by the one still able to keep its feet.

The cheated spectators balled their betting papers and threw them into the pit, falling around the execution scene, the one-eyed cock on his back, his brother trampling and slashing, steel spurs slicing through soft breast feathers, tearing the flesh beneath. Gouts of blood reddened the sand and splashed the onlookers at the edge of the pit but they didn't notice. They were spellbound, exhilarated by the blood-letting and screamed for more.

The crippled cock refused to lie quiet and die quickly. He fought on, striking upwards with spurs that could only do harm with downward strokes and was suffering for it, spending the last of his strength to no purpose. His brother sensed it and paused in his work to crow victory, but too soon. While he crowed the other regained his feet. He was now back in the fight with odds 100-6 against and stood to face attack. Again it came from the air, the crower flying in and then coming down with legs well forward, spurs at an angle that would drive them into the other's skull. But the contact was not made. The one-eyed cock through a quick movement of the head caused the apparent victor to miss and he landed on the bloodied sand, slipped and his comb was seized. If the hold could be kept he was helpless, unable to use beak or spurs, every movement made an injury to himself. But his brother was also bleeding from the empty eye socket and they weakened together, their legs slowly folding under them like concertinas.

When they settled on the floor the comb hold broke and the contest recommenced. They stabbed each other with their beaks, still strong enough to do this if not to support their own weight. The close quarter sparring was deadly and within minutes the odds had changed again. The one-eyed bird had a swollen head, the result of accurate strikes, and it seemed that the game was up for him. Then he got lucky again, striking out and piercing his opponent's left eye, the beak going on into the brain, so far that it was difficult to withdraw. But it was and he struck again at the remaining eye, impaling it and pulling it out, the empty socket dribbling out what remained. His brother was now helpless before him and waited silently for death, head bowed, inviting the final blow.

But the victor was not in a hurry and on regaining his feet crowed his power, savouring the moment, circling his defeated opponent, wings spread, the tips touching the floor. He clucked with pleasure, going around and around, sure of the end and prolonging it, a child with a fly.

He went left about, not the usual way, but he no longer had an eye on that side and was extemporising. He circled many times before at last, satisfied that it was time to end the celebration, he killed, flying into the air and coming down like a thunderbolt on the waiting head, splattering it to every quarter of the pit. The vanquished, headless, moved in frantic spasms then gave up the ghost, at last lying still, an untidy heap of feathers on the trampled sand. The victor stood high on his legs, stretched his swollen head as far as he was able to and crowed again. The last note had barely faded when the owner entered the pit, gathered it up, examined it and wrung its neck. Then he threw the body to the ground.

His action maddened me and I fought an urge to rush to the pit and punish him for this barbarity. I was sick at heart, and for a moment was lost in a despairing reverie, thinking of the unfairness of such a reward for victory. When I returned to myself and looked down to the pit, I saw that there was a crowd of people in it, Trela in the middle, laying about to effect. He had acted while I was indulging in self pity. I went down and joined him.

Between us we cleared the space and looked around for more but there were none, the spectators happy to spectate, view an extra attraction without extra charge. We had only had to deal with the owner, his friends and the pit attendants and could have managed more but there were no more on offer and we left the place.

We cleaned ourselves up at the UJC and then had a drink. Trela wanted to know more about the game and why things had happened as they did.

'It was about money. The bird was killed because it had become an idle mouth. It lost an eye and a one-eyed bird will never win a match against a whole fit one. So the moment its eye was lost its life was lost, worth only the time that remained of the fight.'

'But what about breeding, it would be alright for that?'

'Maybe, maybe not, it would be chancy and the owner was not the sort to take chances. He possibly has the pair that it came from anyway and having hatched two good ones they would hatch others.'

'As good as the one he strangled in the pit?'

'I don't know, nothing is guaranteed.'

Trela went quiet, thinking about it. Would birds like those ever be matched in the future? The contest had gone on for an incredible hour and neither bird had uttered a sound of complaint or given an inch of ground. Both were worth a fortune and that puzzled me. What made the Malay act so hastily and so foolishly in killing the winner without thinking of the possibility of getting others by it? If it bred true he would quickly have become a very rich man. Both birds had been very special. Now they were gone.

Trela no longer saw the Malays as gentle, polite people but as people capable of as much savagery as any other. One of his fondest beliefs had been up-ended and he was perplexed. We remained in the club for another hour and then I left to get the bus to Kota Tinggi. Matt insisted on paying the fare and I was not in the mood to argue; it would be nice to travel in luxury. The passengers on the bus were a mixed bag, farmers with goods bought from the proceeds of vegetables sold, sharp-faced wide boys with caged fowl, peasant women with empty baskets and laps full of children. There were all sorts and many races, Tamils, Chinese, Malays, Sikhs, Eurasians, Javanese, even a Japanese. How had he come to be on board? For all their differences they crowded together in harmony, a babel of people and languages and not one angry voice in the whole crush.

When I left the bus at Johore Bahru, traffic was light with none going to Kota Tinggi. The hope of getting a lift was not very good but I waited for an hour or so anyway. Then I gave up and made my way to Majeeda barracks where I was given a billet for the night. It was in the guardroom manned by cockney RPs. Like most non-Londoners in the army I had a preconceived idea about cockneys and it wasn't a flattering one – though to be fair to them not entirely rational either. I had no first-hand knowledge but now with a chance to gain some was reluctant to do so. Yet I had been quite happy to listen to the tales told about them. They were clannish, tight-fisted, hard to get along with, putting themselves first and everyone else nowhere. They had given me a bed for the night but I was determined that I was not going to enjoy my stay with them – but I did.

They shared their supper with me that night, speaking in a quiet, friendly way throughout the meal. Afterwards I was invited to the wet canteen where I had as much beer as I could face and was not allowed to pay for a drop –'Your money's no good Pat, put it away.' We talked about many things though mainly about horses, greyhounds and racing at Epsom, Catford and White City. They were very knowledgeable and I learned a lot about the subject, particularly the gambling aspect, enough to make me re-think my views on the matter.

Halfway through the evening three of the RPs joined a card game and I watched for a while. They were good, winning consistently and I wondered how they would manage in a game run by 'Colonel' Cambell, D Squadron's card sharp. I could imagine him sitting down to a friendly game with them. Greek meeting Greeks. It would be a game well worth watching if not being part of.

On the following morning, to further confound my previous view, the provost sergeant, who had not been in the guardroom overnight, offered me a lift to the signals school. It was out of his way and I refused. It would be easy to get a lift at that time of day anyway and it wouldn't be right to waste so much of his time. But he insisted and I had to accept. He was also a cockney hailing from a place he referred to as the Isle of Dogs, a district of London far from the countryside. Yet that seemed to be his main interest in life and during the journey he gave a resumé of the history of agriculture in Kent and had started a monologue on the finer points of hop-picking between the wars when we arrived at the school and it had to come to an end. Before leaving he gave me an invitation to visit Majeeda any-time I was in the vicinity and I accepted. I had to find out the difference between female and male hops – he had mentioned it but the journey ended before he could elaborate.

16

MIN YAH AND FIGHT NIGHT

Life at Kota Tinggi was humdrum, tranquil as the reading room of a public library, but occasionally there would be moments of excitement. On 12 November, shots were fired on the camp perimeter, close to our basha. There were just three of us in the barrack room at the time and we went out to investigate. The night was pitch black but I had a torch and when we got to the wire, used it to search for breaks. It was an unusual way to proceed knowing that whoever had fired the shots might well have done so to lure targets, but it was the only way, hazardous or otherwise. After following the wire for about 200 yards we found a hole large enough for a man to squeeze through. After searching the immediate area we continued the search on the outside of the wire, going north towards the guardroom. The guard had not turned out so it was unlikely that the shots had been heard by them, but there was a possibility that they had and if so they would be playing possum, waiting to blaze away at anything that moved and we were moving in a free fire zone, likely targets for both sentries and insurgents.

To lessen the chance of being shot by the sentries I sent Hendry back through the wire to let the guard commander know what we were doing and which way we were moving. Just after he had gone there was a sound to our front and we halted, listening, hoping to pinpoint the spot it had come from. But there was only silence and after a while Gallagher fired a short burst, low, clearing the ground in front of us. Then we continued towards the guardroom and were about 50 yards from it when a fusillade of bullets cracked around us, coming from inside the camp. Hendry had not made it to the guardroom in time. On seeing the muzzle flashes I'd gone to ground faster than a prairie dog and Gallagher was not far behind me. He started to swear as soon as he hit the ground and with some style. The sentries were not impressed and continued zipping bullets at us. Fortunately for us if not for their chance of becoming old soldiers they kept them at waist level and they passed harmlessly over our heads. Gallagher roared for some time before the firing at last died down to ragged volleys and then stopped. We made the most of the opportunity, getting to our feet as quickly as we could and making it to the guardroom in record time. Hendry was already there and when he saw us, laughed like a jackass. Gallagher was for killing him on the spot and that brought the laughter to a close. I asked him why he had not passed the message to the guard commander.

'I did.'

'Then why were we fired on?'

'I don't know, I gave him the message.'

'What was the message?'

'That you were coming from the north.'

'Coming from the north? You bloody fool, going north, north, not bloody south. No wonder we were fired on. You could have got us killed.'

When I paused for breath, Gallagher who had remained silent during the exchange started to swear again, saying most of the things I had missed out. His words calmed me at a moment when I was about to make a serious attempt on Hendry's life. Instead I swore again starting when Gallagher stopped, stringing together a satisfying number of oaths, threats and dire promises. They went on long enough to dismiss any lingering thought or design I had about taking life.

When tempers cooled without blows being exchanged we sat down to a late night supper courtesy of the guard commander. It was small compensation considering what had happened half an hour earlier. The meal commenced in silence but fairly soon we came around and started to talk, appreciating the humour of the ludicrous happenings of the night, laughing about them, allowing Hendry to join in without penalty. We were signallers playing at soldiers.

Towards the end of November the class, well advanced on the course, was rewarded with five days of leave. I decided to spend it in Singapore. I could afford to, the pay-master for one reason or another paying me as a single man without dependents and therefore without deductions. It was the first time it had happened in over eighteen months and I was more than pleased. Suddenly I was rich and put aside all other concerns, even Lionel the tax inspector. He was still pursuing me, sending begging letters every week and others threatening me with bankruptcy proceedings unless I coughed up. He had a bulldog quality that appealed to me and I was beginning to be very fond of him.

On arrival in Singapore I was still feeling rich and booked in at the Sandes Club. It was, in the words of the advert 'well-appointed' – and fairly expensive. It was also handy for the city centre and the various meeting places of the Regiment so the expense was worthwhile.

That evening I met Jock Taylor in the UJC. He was not in the best of humours, his face a passable imitation of a funeral director's mute, but after a few drinks he picked up, cracked his face and started to moan. The Regiment, in his estimation, was going down the drain. Petty discipline was the order of the day and charge sheets were flying around Selarang like confetti, the slightest infringement of KRRs meriting punishment. Jock Smith was on orders for failing to salute an officer. Calvert had never made

Endless drilling in Singapore.

saluting an issue and it was hard to accept that what had once been a matter of choice was now an obligation. It was now clear even to the dimmest that the purpose of the move to Singapore was not for training or reequipping but for disciplinary reasons. The free spirits were to be drilled into the iron-discipline of the barrack square. That had to be so when saluting was seen as more important than bushcraft or skill at arms. Initiative was being squeezed out of the men and mediocrity phased in. It seemed that Calvert's dream of a regiment where worth was paramount was fading and he was helpless to stop the process.

Jock had spoken quickly, with urgency up to the point where Calvert came into the story, then he paused for a while. When he went on it was obvious that he was choked by the way things were and dwelling on them made it worse. I changed the subject, suggesting a move, and he agreed.

The atmosphere in The Happy Word was to his liking and we stayed for an hour before moving, going to his favourite haunt down by the harbour. It was a tiny place with few customers but the same beer was served there as anywhere else so it suited very well. Two Chinese girls came into the bar soon after our arrival and Jock spoke to them and then brought them over and introduced us. They were old friends of his and looking at them I could understand his reason for keeping them a secret for so long. They were beautiful, one outstandingly so. She smiled when I took her hand but did not speak and remained silent after we sat down. It was hard to take my eyes away from her, she moved like a cat and looked like Myrna Loy plus, very special. But why the silence?

Later, when she left the table for a moment, Jock told me. She had no tongue. His words were devastating and when she returned I was unsure of how to react to the changed situation. She was still beautiful but I could only think of a disfigurement that could not be seen. How could perception be changed so quickly without visible cause? I had admired her as a woman but could now only pity her as something less. She noticed but made little of it, smiling more. After a while everything was almost as it had been and we talked. She understood everything I said and replied with signs, her friend interpreting. It was all very pleasant after my awkwardness had passed.

As the evening went on I got to know a lot about her. When the Japanese had occupied Singapore nine years earlier she had been arrested for aiding a Chinese resistance group, and was held in Changi jail for questioning. The questioning went on for three days but failed to elicit any answers. Typically, the Japanese having failed to make her speak, ensured that she never would. Her tongue was impaled on a spike, pulled out to its full extent and slashed through the root with a cutthroat razor. Afterwards she was thrown unconscious into a bare, windowless cell. She would now either bleed to death or choke on her own blood, but did not, miraculously surviving. During the following three years she wished many times that she had not, her captors subjecting her to unimaginable tortures. In all that time she never saw the light of day.

She was freed after the defeat of the Japanese in 1945 and for the first few weeks was blind as well as mute. When her sight returned she was terrified to see armed Japanese soldiers still patrolling the streets. Had they really lost the war? It seemed that they were needed to keep order in the city, but under the control of the British.

'But why are they not being punished?'

After recovering her sight she worked as a sew-sew girl but after a while her eyes weakened again and she was unable to carry on. Then, without any other prospects she became a taxi dancer and that was how she now earned a living.

Her name was Min-Yah but her clients called her Dum-Dum. There was no hurt intended, but she was hurt and it was with her all the time. It made her tense, frightened and yet she still smiled and believed that we were good men. She was very young looking; the Japanese had imprisoned her when she was fifteen and now nine years later she still appeared to be the same age. But though she smiled a lot she never laughed. That was their legacy to her.

Min Yah was not compensated for her injury or her long years of suffering in Changi and with the war over she was forgotten. When I got Jock on his own I asked him what he thought about it all. He was not impressed.

'It's just a yarn,' he said, 'they tell you anything. Forget it.'

But I could not. I believed the girl. She didn't have a tongue; that was a fact. Jock had insinuated that she was a liar and that posed the question, how did she lose her tongue if not in the way her friend said? Had she cut it out herself to elicit sympathy? That was almost unthinkable. She was young and very beautiful and in the east, even more so than in the west, those attributes added up to a passport to an easy life. But for all her good looks and youth she was, in the eyes of her peers, disfigured. She could never hope for a husband, yet if whole her choices would have been limitless.

Her terrible story had sobered me and I decided to make my way back to the Sandes Club for an earlier than expected end to the evening. I shook hands with both girls before leaving and gave what money I had to Min Yah, my personal payment of compensation. It amounted to less than three weeks' pay but she reacted to the gift as if it had been a fortune. Jock was staying on and I left on my own for the walk back to the club.

Next morning I got ready to return to Kota Tinggi. I was broke, having disposed of five days' ration money and three weeks' pay in the space of twelve hours. It had to be some sort of record. Half an hour after rising I was on the road. Traffic was light but I managed to get a lift and was back at the signal school by noon.

That night there was another shooting incident on the perimeter wire but with a vivid recollection of the last one, at first I decided to pass this time around. But the firing persisted and I thought that it might be worth a look after all, anything to pass the night on. When I got there the action was taking place, not on the wire but on the road running past the camp, a number of RPs blazing away with sten guns, pumping hundreds of bullets into the darkness. They were firing, one said, in the direction taken by six 'bandits' who had crossed the road ten minutes earlier heading for the belukar beyond it. I believed him and said that by now they would have moved on a bit, along the tree line parallel to the road. Why not change aim, firing along their escape route instead of the place they had last been seen? By now, unless they were playing possum, they would be half a mile away, making the best of their way home.

The RPs listened but ignored the advice and continued to fire into the belukar, unwilling to believe that it was difficult to get through in daylight and impossible at night. Having failed to convince them I decided to show them the way by example, setting off at a trot along the road, making up for the quarry's head start. After travelling about 800 yards I stopped and put a couple of shots into the scrub. There was no return and I tried a few along the line of belukar allowing for the angle between the road and the trees. After getting two magazines away I was joined by the RPs who were quickly zipping bursts in the same general direction; it was returned. There were no muzzle flashes, only the crack of bullets, passing us by without harm and the sharp bang when others were fired, .303s for a certainty. They gave away the position of those firing them, 150 yards ahead, out of range of the sten guns. We moved on 100 yards and concentrated fire. The RPs fired in the right direction but high, dangerous only to low flying aircraft. When the aim was lowered it was too low, ploughing the ground 25 yards to our front, daisy cutting. Fairly soon they ran out of ammunition.

For once all the men are in official attire, a tall order for the free-willed members of the regiment.

I was relieved. There was now little chance of being killed by them, their skill at arms comparable only to the Japanese who, when armed and angry, are dangerous to everyone except those standing directly in front of them.

In any event, ammunition aside, it was plain that we had missed the main chance and the apprentice Nimrods fell back to the guardroom. There, supper having been disposed of, we supped tea and the RPs reminisced about the night's happening. Listening to them I had no doubt that within a week or so they would be comparing it to the July offensive on the Somme.

About a week after the shoot-out a battalion of the King's African Rifles arrived at the school. It was assumed by many, with events of the recent past in mind, that they were to take responsibility for camp security but it was not the case. They were there to be trained in the art of jungle warfare and early in the following year would carry out their first operation role in the campaign in the company of elements of D Squadron, myself included. I took a particular interest in them. They were the first black troops I had been in contact with other than a service battalion of Mauritians met up with during service in Egypt. The Mauritians alas, had been cut to size by the system making them less; the Africans had not and were keen and able soldiers. It was not surprising to find that the majority of the warrant officers and senior NCOs had soldiered with Calvert's Brigade in the Chindit campaign in Burma. The regiment had served with distinction there, particularly so in the savage hand to hand fighting that had taken place around the fortified camps of Broadway and White City. It was a small world. But I had little to do with them, at least for now. I was still at school, being taught things I already knew.

Sergeant Tattersall looked upon R/T sets as members of his family, to be looked after and cherished, particularly if new. Before being issued for field use, new sets had to be tested and towards the end of the course he entrusted the task to me. It was, as Hendry said with a rare flash of wit, a signal honour.

The test was not involved, simply sending and receiving messages in code and en clair from a distance of 20 miles or so. The chosen test place was Gilman barracks, which though pleasant enough, did not suit my plans for the day and I suggested Selarang. Tattersall, an NCO of the old school, confident enough to change his mind and give the horse its head now and again, agreed.

I arrived at Selarang at 7.30am the following morning and set up on the highest ground in the barracks, close by the officer's mess, the best reception area. The results of the test from such a position would be excellent, if of little use in evaluating the worth of the set when used operationally. I had selected the site to demonstrate this obvious oversight; the sets would be used in the jungle and the jungle was the proper place to test them. The chance that they would fail once in the rainforest seemed pretty high. The test-

ing of R/T sets on delivery to the army was agreed jointly by the War Office and agents of the manufacturers. The terms were loaded in favour of the makers; here I was testing kit that was supposedly field worthy in almost sterile conditions. I could complain about it, but would be marked down as a barrack room lawyer for my pains. Sergeant Tattersall could do so, ensuring that he would be passed over for further promotion, even leaving himself open to breaking. But the complaint had to be made, even if only by my choice of test site.

An hour after opening the net Major Woodhouse put in an appearance, heading for a late breakfast. With the example of Jock Smith in mind I made a point of giving him an extra snappy salute. He noticed and made a point of being off-hand in his return. We were still sparring and he was still getting the best of it. He had a look at the set and then at me.

Major John Woodhouse in full uniform.

our way to the wash house to clean up I looked at the watch on my left wrist; it said 1.15pm. We had gone at it for over an hour.

'Do you remember the cock fight Matt?'

'Well it wasn't long ago, why do you ask?'

'It was the longest match ever, a record, and we beat it by five minutes.'

'Yea, but we're not chickens are we and no bastard broke our necks at the end.' That was true and I could not argue. He had a long memory and I hoped that he would never again meet up with the fellow who had killed the winner of the first cockfight he'd ever seen. His tooth remained in my forehead, a lump between flesh and bone but with no great loss of blood, which was odd. The entry hole was a quarter of an inch wide, plenty of space for a gusher. I removed it in the wash house aided by two of the fight fans, one holding a mirror, the other giving advice. The tooth was well down under unbroken skin. I worked it out as if cording a curtain but in reverse. That night I returned it to its owner. He and I and others were gathered around the water tanks discussing the events of the day and Daisy the cocker spaniel had just made her umpteenth delivery of Tiger beer. It was a most auspicious moment, the kicker accepting his tooth in the manner of a staff officer accepting the OBE. He had style. I'd thought that when he put me down in the ruck. While I lay on the ground wondering where his boot would land, my kidneys, head, stomach or small of the back, he circled, taking his time, keeping me in suspense. I guessed the head. It was the shins. He not only had style but was a tactician.

Back in the barrack room there was a better feeling in the air. The men were talking to each other again, sure of themselves, confident. They had just witnessed a demonstration of the value of the individual, a value fostered by Calvert. It was a reminder of better times and it cheered them. He had told them that they were not chessmen to be moved around a board as a caprice but 'counter-guerrillas who move after due consideration within the group.' They had believed that then and would come back to belief, their importance only forgotten for the one moment.

17

THE PHANTOM ORGANIST

After the contest I rested on Trela's bunk and without meaning to nodded off. It was 4.00pm when I woke, sore all over, my left ear ringing, right eye closed up and a fair number of teeth missing, with others loose at their moorings. My upper lip was cut through to the gum but had stopped bleeding. It was too late to get it stitched and that meant a scar when it came together. My ribcage was blotched red and the bones ached. Otherwise, as McDonald would say, I was fine.

But fine or otherwise I had a problem with the R/T set and Sergeant Tattersall. I had not sent or received any messages for four hours though the net had been open and that meant that the batteries would be run down. He would want an explanation of that and for the change in my appearance since that morning. The explanation would have to be good and I wondered if I had enough time to come up with a tale that he would not find too difficult to swallow. After consideration I was forced to conclude that there was no excuse for leaving the set and the only one I could think of to explain my injuries was that I had fallen off the back of a lorry, an unlikely tale.

On the way back to Kota Tinggi I tried for a more plausible yarn but without success and on arrival that remained the state of play. In the circumstances I was not in a hurry to report my safe return. That, as it turned out was just as well for the news of the day had preceded me – everyone knew and that being the case Tattersall would not have appreciated my fairytale version of events. They knew because I had left the set netted into not only the school but also to Majeeda and Gilman barracks. In my absence someone – 'Colonel' Cambell if rumour was to be believed – had taken advantage of the situation and became a radio broadcaster, giving a blow by blow account of the match to attentive audiences all over Malaya.

Sergeant Tattersall had listened in from the beginning, recording every word of the broadcast in Pitman's shorthand – filling five pages of a message pad. Would a military court accept that as evidence? Only if put forward and if I knew my man he would not do that. He was not as concerned about the set as I had imagined either; perhaps he did not look on it as family after all. He was concerned about my state of health and told Hendry to take me to the RAP but I refused to go. The MO would not be as accommodating as he had been and would certainly make a report on the matter which would go up the line and result in action being taken against both Trela and myself. He accepted that and did not press the matter. In any case I thought I would be alright by morning; as it turned out Tattersall was right about seeking medical attention, as would soon become apparent. When leaving he put a hand on my shoulder and asked if I would reconsider going to the RAP, but on my refusal wished me well and left it at that.

On the way to the barrack room I gave some thought to Sergeant Tattersall and his way of going about things. I liked his style: no fuss, no bull, a real professional. He had stuck his neck out for me and instead of letting me know all about it had welcomed me like a prodigal son and wished me well. A rare bird. It was 7.00pm when I got to the basha but in spite of the early hour and the afternoon's rest I was tired out and turned in straight away. As soon as my head was down I was asleep and dreaming, or something like that. In my nightmares I was in a swamp and felt the mud close over my head and I kept still, slowing my descent into the depths, hoping that some part of me, some part of my Bergen, would still be showing when the next man in the column came upon the scene. He did not come and I continued down, clamping my lips against the mud and went into blackness.

I awoke in a different place, in a bed with a white pillow and sheets. It was very comfortable, far superior to the one I had got into – and it got better. Beside the bed was a very pretty woman. She was holding my left wrist in one hand and stroking my fevered brow with the other. For a while she did not notice that I was awake and continued holding and stroking. Not wanting to interfere with or hamper what was obviously important work I continued to play possum. But all good things come to an end. She noticed my sly looks, stopped stroking and started talking.

I'd been brought into the hospital early that morning accompanied by Private Mott. On his return to the basha around 11.30pm on the previous evening he had noticed that I was breathing unevenly and on taking a closer look saw that my face had turned blue. He woke Hendry who went to the RAP to contact the MO, who on arrival rendered first aid and then rushed me to hospital, the 'bon mott' riding shotgun.

My problems had arisen due to a lack of air, caused by blood hardening in the nose, complicated when the cut in my upper lip opened and started bleeding again, blocking my windpipe. When Mott appeared on the scene I was quietly, or fairly quietly, dying of suffocation.

'Why was I going so quietly?'

'Some do, some don't. You had lost a lot of blood. No, don't tell me how you lost it, everybody in Singapore knows, so don't try and come the clever clogs.'

'I wasn't going to say a word about it.'

'No, well perhaps not, anyway the loss made you too weak to struggle or even wake up.'

'What if I say I won't struggle now?'

'Don't even think about it. You are ill and will be here for some time.'

I looked at her, wondering what she would say if I asked her what I was not to think about but decided against. The 'some time' was a prospect to anticipate and I did not want to spoil my chances by getting her back up in the early stages of the game. She was something to write home about, a reincarnation of the goddess Juno in fancy dress.

On examination later that morning three cracked ribs were added to my list of injuries and I thought about persuading Trela to take up a career in the ring. He had the punching ability of Jack Dempsey and with the right trainer and manager could well become cruiserweight champion of the world, my upper lip an earnest of that. As thought, it had been left too long for stitching and 'Juno' drew it together with elastoplasts. She also pulled two loose teeth; the others would firm up she said. All I had to do now was to stay in bed and behave myself. That did not appeal but I had companions in adversity, about 30 men from the four operational SAS squadrons, most of them in poor shape. Ten had been that way for a month or more.

My strength came back quickly. Eating while doing nothing to earn it tends to have that effect. Nurse 'Juno' helped and during the times she was absent from the ward I would also leave and visit, sitting beside beds, yammering about the old days in the jungle. Were they eight months ago? We all liked to talk, quickening the time that we wanted to pass. One of my bedfellows, a conscript with Weil's disease, died two days before his nineteenth birthday. A telegram was sent to his family – KIA. On receipt his mother and father would be heartbroken. But what if they had been told of the real way of it? Not a kindly bullet in the head but 33 days of dying, an aeon of pain.

Another man on the ward, Trooper Stanley, was good in situations like that, as one with us though not of us, a wry, impish Irishman, popular with everyone. When the conscript died he geed us out of self pity by showing us another facet of hospital death, the end of a tapeworm. The worm had been in the stomach of a young soldier for a long time, eating everything he ate and making a living skeleton of him in the process. Stanley took us to his bedside. He had fasted for three days and the worm was very hungry, ready to travel for a meal. A plate of milk and oatmeal was placed by the soldier's head and gradually the worm left the stomach, coming out through the open mouth to eat in light what had been denied in darkness. It was 24 inches long and it was vital that no segment remaining in the man's body, as if one tiny fragment of it returned to the stomach it would grow again. When well out into the open Stanley closed the mouth of its host and Trooper Murray scooped the parasite into a jar and sealed it away. Entertaining though the process had been, it was not quite enough to compensate for seeing death from ratcatcher's yellow.

Being in hospital is fine so long as one is out within a week. After that the routine becomes a relentless monotony, unbearable without distraction, frisky nurses, the occasional sip of smuggled beer, storytelling. I and my fellows were also distracted by something far less pleasant, a being we termed the Phantom Organist.

He, she or it performed every day promptly at 1.00pm, shattering, ponderous notes coming through the ward's ceiling from the room directly overhead. It was like a daily funeral march, doing no good to those men hanging between life and death. No one fully believed that the performer was human, as even though a watch was sited at every entrance to the organ room, no one was ever seen entering. We only knew that they had slipped past us when the first chords reverberated round the hospital.

The noise was such that everyone complained but nothing was done. Speculation began. 'It' was the Senior Medical Officer. Who would dare to interfere with his amusement? But if so, what was the reason for his manic recitals? Many conjectured that he was playing out of unrequited love, perhaps for the matron, who they imagined had spurned him for another man. Others said that the organist was the matron herself, spurned by the SMO and therefore taking her revenge using the organ as her weapon of reprisal. They supported this claim by pointing out that the recitals were orchestrated to cause the greatest alarm and despondency amongst the patients, hampering their recovery and in some cases halting it altogether. It was a state of affairs calculated to cast doubt on the professional competence of the SMO. The fury of a woman scorned is not to be taken lightly.

Efforts to catch the Phantom in the act all ended in failure, so it was decided to destroy the organ itself. Herculean efforts were made to that end but they failed miserably. All doors leading to the first floor of the building, the lair of the instrument, were iron-clad and bolted, and no attempts to break through or pick the locks were successful. But they were watched every day by men keen to bring an end to the general suffering, hoping to nail the Phantom on the way to the instrument when the door was unlocked, break through to the loft and do for the instrument. But none of the doors were ever opened. Clearly the Phantom was getting to the instrument by other means, perhaps through a window? That let the matron off the hook. There wasn't a window in the place large enough for her to get through. It also cleared the SMO, if only from entry in that particular way, as he got dizzy looking down at his boots. He clearly had another, undiscovered point of access. So the recitals continued and the patients languished. Then the SMO got a phone call from a mysterious man who would not give his name. Stop the music or else. That did the trick and the daily recitals ended, saving many lives, his included.

On 3 December Woodhouse paid us a visit at the hospital and was welcomed by all. After the preliminaries he told us that parachute training was to begin shortly and that the Regiment was to remain in Singapore for the foreseeable future. Good news as far as he was concerned, but most of us disagreed. There was no point parachuting in a forested country like Malaya unless bent on self destruction by impalement, and the promised long stay in Singapore was a breach of our terms of service. When he left there were many raised voices in the ward, most of them condemning the future he had outlined for us.

Two days after his visit I was fit enough to be discharged and had mixed feelings about it; glad I was going, sorry that I had to leave so many friends behind me. The

SMO had a word before I left. He was pleased with my rapid recovery and having said so wished me well for the future. I thanked him for his good wishes, hoping that he didn't recognise my voice from the phone call that had ended his lunchtime frolics in the organ loft.

I got a lift back to Kota Tinggi in a jeep driven by a lieutenant in the KARs. He was a man in a hurry and believed that slow was sure but that speed was surer and the jeep was driven around every corner on two wheels in order to demonstrate the validity of his theory. Against all the odds we arrived at the school without overturning and in record time. The only fault was that every millimetre of tread had been stripped from the tyres. Maybe he had the offer of a job from Pirelli on completion of service. There was no doubt that he was capable of testing their product to destruction in half the time it normally took, which would be a definite asset in that line of work.

The meeting of the ad hoc committee arranged for 19 December took place in The Happy Word. Mr Lam had set aside a room for our use and everyone was present by 8.00pm. There was only one matter for discussion: the round robin. The urgency of its implementation was made clear from the beginning of the meeting, increased by the news that the Regiment was to remain on the island indefinitely. It was just one of the many decisions directly affecting the ORs in which they had no say, and we had to make our views known.

Colonel Calvert no longer had any say in the Regiment and there was a rumour circulating that he had been removed from command against his will. Officially he was suffering from a tropical disease, but few of us believed this. The mosquitoes that bit him did not give him malaria, they got it. So what was the point of the official version of his state of health and how did it fit in with the report put to the meeting that for the past three months he had led a very active life, riding every morning and playing golf every afternoon? It didn't fit and fooled few. Who had thought that it would? Those with a low opinion of the intellect of the rank and file. No one in authority, other than Calvert, seemed to be aware of the calibre of the men in the Regiment.

At 9.00pm it was agreed that the round robin should go forward, after a unanimous vote by all twelve of us present. The wording was then discussed, agreed and drawn up. Before being passed for signing it was made plain that those doing so would be acting in breach of KRRs and be liable to court-martial as soon as their names were appended – if discovered at an inopportune time. All signed. Protection from court-martial would come by degrees. The more signatures the less chance of a court. Twelve men would be charged and tried, 50 would not. If and when that number had committed themselves the RR would be put before the acting CO for consideration.

The final draft of the round robin requested that the principles on which the Regiment was founded be reinstated. That the implicit contracts of the volunteers be honoured. That the Regiment return to the war up-country. And that the rank and file be informed and consulted on matters directly concerning them. It was short and to the point, yet contained the main concerns of the men, drawn up in good faith. The physical existence of the paper was of course the weak link in the chain and further signatures would have to be got with discretion. Canvassers would be just that, the paper held by another, to be produced when the bona-fides of would-be signatories had been accepted. The meeting closed at 9.30pm.

Later that night I treated Matt Trela to a few drinks. It was the least I could do, as he had visited me every day I'd been in hospital. How he managed it was a mystery. Transport into the city would have cost him most of his pay. We remained in the bar until 11.00pm and then I left to return to Kota Tinggi.

Outside the Union Jack Club a 3-ton truck was parked up, the back full of BORs, most of them from the school. One waved me over, making room for me by the tailgate. The truck would be leaving for Kota Tinggi shortly. Just before it did a Malay spoke to the driver and then came to the back of the truck and spoke to us. We would have to get off; the truck was for the use of Malays only. I didn't like his attitude and told the men to stay where they were. The Malay turned to me.

'You must order them to get off. I am an officer and I am ordering you to do so.'

I looked at him and was not impressed. There was no way that I was going to ask BORs to make way for little fellows in snow-white trousers, dinky velour blouses and black velvet Cossack hats.

'You have no authority to order me to do anything. Now go away.' But he didn't, instead speaking to the men.

'Come on, all of you get off.' His lisped words were barely loud enough to be heard inside the truck but in case they were I told the men to stay put. Then I turned to the Malay.

'Look, this is a British Army truck with British soldiers aboard. None of them are getting off; I will not allow them to. Now go away.' But he stayed and now produced a sheet of paper which he looked at for some seconds before passing it to me. It was authority for the use of the truck reserving it for Malays – in Jawi script. I gave it back to him. 'What is this, why have you given it to me?'

'It is an order for the use of the truck.'

'Right, so we are using it.'

'It is not authorised for your use.'

'I don't need authorisation to use it.'

'The order says Malays only.'

'That bit of paper says nothing, it is you that is saying. We are on and are staying on.'

At that he left and I told the driver to move off. He started the engine but before he got it into gear the Malay returned with two regimental policemen who confirmed the order and ordered us off. But how had they been able to confirm it? I asked the sergeant to translate but he couldn't and I told the men to stay where they were. The other red-cap did not like that and shouted. He was pushing his luck.

'Nobody is getting off. I'll not walk while they ride.' But he insisted and after a lot of language the men got off and drifted away. I was disappointed. They had allowed themselves to be bested in a confrontation they could have won by just sitting tight and doing nothing.

I remained on the truck and was joined by one of the red-caps. He took hold of my arm.

'Right, come on.'

'If you want me off you'd better call your mates to give you a lift.'

'Come on, you're being a fool.'

'No, there is no way I'm getting off. You're showing preference to them over us and I'm not having it. What would you have done if it had been the other way round, would you have thrown them off so that we could take their place?' That changed his mood and he became conciliatory.

'Look I will ask if you can travel with them, OK?'

'Yeah, if they are willing to travel with me I have no objections to travelling with them.'

At that he left and spoke to the officer and came back smiling. He had obviously successfully completed a delicate diplomatic exchange.

'Everything's OK. I've fixed it, you can stay on.' It was plain that he was very pleased with himself and I didn't want to spoil it with any outright sarcasm so I just thanked him and left it at that.

The incident clearly illustrated the second rate status that BORs were being increasingly forced to accept. It had nothing to do with the Malays so much as the white hoi-poloi who, while wishing to ingratiate themselves generally, did not want their supposed superiority over other races, particularly the Malays, to be watered down by frequent contact between British and Malay soldiers. It was an attitude shared by the army top brass who were prepared to see BORs as second rate if that helped to retain what they and the tuans saw as the status quo.

The journey to the mainland was enjoyable and instructive, the Malays, for all my imagined perceptions much the same as all soldiers. They laughed and talked a lot about unimportant things, speaking on important ones in a shorthand of expletives. They were polite, those I spoke to making great efforts to comprehend my inimitable version of their language, only laughing when I described their officer as an old man of the woods.

'No,' one said, 'The young man of the kampongs.'

That caused general amusement but I missed the point and could not join in. Grammar was not one of my strong points and the use of inflexion to change the meaning of words was a closed book to me. When the journey ended I was genuinely sorry to leave their company.

18

CHRISTMAS GIFTS AND THE BLEATING OF POLES

20 December was the last day of the signals course and also my birthday. As in past years I received a cake from home, a magnificent creation, my name, age and a birthday wish trailed across it in icing sugar. The candles, all 22 of them, were packed separately, and I stowed the parcel away under my bunk until the celebration in the canteen planned for that night. In the meantime I had to take the signals tests.

The tests went on all day and at the end of it we returned to the basha to compare positions on the ratings list. I was not particularly concerned about my place and decided that now was as good a time as any to take my cake to the canteen. I reached for it under the bunk and failing to find it, got on my knees to look. There was nothing there. Someone had lifted it while we were busy splicing wires and sending complicated messages to each other. Who could have taken it? There were no loose-wallas in the area and stealing from our particular basha was considered to be a very hazardous business indeed, the occupants having a reputation for deeds before words. But reputation or not it had still gone. It was a mystery but there could be none about its disposal. By now the thief would have eaten it and the central attraction of the evening was no more. That being the case I decided to call it a day; a birthday party without a cake would be like a wedding night without a bride.

I was fed up with parties anyway, too old to bother any more and an early night would serve me better. The basha was now deserted, the graduates in the wet canteen celebrating success or drowning their sorrows. It was the first time I'd been alone in the barrack room since returning early from leave a month before and there was a strange quietness in the air. It was very pleasant and I lay in the darkness thinking of other times, 1945 and my first birthday in the army. I was sixteen then and billeted at Hardwick Hall in Derbyshire. That had been a very special day, the party starting in the Kit-bag Club in Chesterfield and continuing in a miner's cottage on the outskirts of Mansfield, the front room crowded with people. And what people! Pleasant and hospitable, not at odds with themselves or with us, a rare experience. In other places we were seen as a threat, though what we were supposed to threaten was never made clear. The attitude was marked during our stay on the Isle of Wight causing me to wonder if, like the Channel Islanders, they preferred German to British troops.

I was dozing off when the light went on and Gallagher, Hendry and the Bon Mott came in. They had been invited to a party and had been waiting in the canteen for it to begin. Why had I not turned up? When I told them they refused to accept it as a reason and insisted that I go.

'We can still have a drink together, cake or no cake, come on.' Gallagher was determined and I stopped making excuses and went with them.

When we got to the canteen Mott and the others stopped just inside the door looking for a vacant table. Then, after a few moments, they went in and I followed. As soon as I was through the door the lights were switched off and the mystery of the cake was solved. There it was, sitting squarely on a table in the centre of the room, all 22 candles lit and shining like beacons in the darkness. Hendry, the cunning Scot had been responsible for its removal aided by Mott and Gallagher and just for the sake of form I tore them off a strip. But it was a waste of time. They were laughing so much that they didn't hear me. I went to the head of the table to begin the night's proceedings. When I blew the candles out there was a bit of a commotion. The switch man had deserted his post and the canteen was in darkness.

I cut the birthday cake before the serious drinking started, which was the safest way. A couple of years earlier an athletic toper had managed to sit on one, flattening the cake and suffering burns to a part of his anatomy which, even after drinking copious draughts of issue rum, he refused to bare for inspection. As the night went on we were joined by others and the inexhaustible beer supply ran out at 2.00am. By then everyone had drunk enough anyway, some, myself included, too much, and when the celebration ended I decided to sleep under the stars. Tiger beer brings out the romantic in many but only serves to make me act foolishly and so, having decided to do otherwise could not be persuaded to sleep in the basha. Instead I found a comfortable-looking grassy hollow, settled down for what remained of the night and was soon asleep. Some time later the heavens opened and I awoke to a deluge, retreating to the barrack room looking like a drowned rat. The celebration was complete. It had been one of the best ever.

On the following day with the course ended, the pupils departed. I arrived at Selarang in the afternoon and after reporting in spoke with one of the committee members. The round robin was doing better than expected, ten more names added in less than two days. At this rate the required 50 would be secured within the week. It was very encouraging and I turned in that night satisfied that at last things were going our way. At 3.00am we were awakened by a very inebriated Corporal Dover, encouraged by Eddy Waters and two other troopers. He was as drunk as a lord and throwing everything movable all over the place.

Being drunk was fine, wrecking the barrack room was not. The rules concerning drink were few: sup until it comes out of the ears but don't impose on others, particularly not in the barracks. Dover had broken the cardinal rule and was shouting loud enough to wake the dead. He had to be stopped for his own good, so I spoke up.

'Hold it down a bit, there's a bloke here on early duties.'

The noise tailed off and he looked at me and then, after drunken deliberation started to shout again, as loud as ever. I thought of putting him in the quadrangle and locking him out for the night but dismissed the idea. He was a good soldier. Once, when parched and too tired to search for water he had given me a drink. Such things cannot be forgotten and are hard to repay. I owed him.

He was acting out of character and there had to be a reason for it. Where was the harm in letting him go on for a while anyway? I'd have a word with him in the morning that would make him think twice before taking liberties in the future. The racket went on for another hour, then, too tired to continue, he flopped on his bunk and went quickly to sleep.

Next morning he was the worse for wear and far from apologetic. When I spoke to him he turned the complaint around, angry with me for interfering in his business.

'Don't piss around with me again or you're in trouble, OK?'

His response angered me but even then I wanted to ignore his threat but could not.

'Right then, but if you break the rules again I'll do more than interfere, got it?'

He rolled into the barrack room with his followers just before midnight and the mayhem began immediately. Empty bunks went over and when the floor was littered they began a mini Grand National over the obstacles. The provocation was studied and served its purpose. Dover had promised me trouble and was now forcing the pace, daring me to interfere. In return I had promised him more than words if he broke the rules again. I should now be making good on that but instead decided to reason with him. The noise was so loud that if it continued would be heard by the orderly officer and investigated. That could cost Dover dearly. If found drunk he would be put under close arrest and he would lose his tapes. I didn't want that to happen. It would be bad news for him and almost as bad for the ORs in general. His high jinks would be put to use as a stick for our backs, yet another example of the drunkenness and ill-discipline that was said to be endemic in the Regiment. The fact that he had been an exemplary NCO up to that point would be ignored.

'The orderly officer is due any minute lads and he'll give you all grief if he finds you like this. Go to bed for awhile, till he's finished his rounds. You'll be alright then.'

They were drunk but not to the extent of the previous night and I thought that they would act on the advice but they didn't. The noise stopped but they remained where they were, like statues. Dover moved. He came up to me, so close that I could barely keep my place, looking into my face. Then he pushed me, hard. Unprepared and off-balance I fell backwards over one of the up-ended bunks. When I got to my feet he made no attempt to hide his amusement. He laughed and his friends joined in. The rest of the men, now out of their bunks, watched and waited on events. McDonald nudged me.

'You want any help Joe?'

'No, I can manage.'

'But you can't let that go.'

'I don't intend to.'

That satisfied him and he gave no more advice. I didn't need any. Dover's action could not be ignored, everyone knew that and what the response should be. But the situation was not straightforward. If I struck him and he pulled rank instead of striking back I would be in trouble. But I could get around that, challenge him to a match on the cobbles. It was the only alternative to a possible charge of striking a superior officer. If he refused he would lose his friends, authority and respect.

He accepted. There was nothing else he could do and we went out to the quadrangle followed by the rest of D Squadron. Dover was big, two inches taller than me and a stone or so heavier. His drunkenness was a handicap but I was not fully recovered from the pounding taken from Trela three weeks before. It was an even match all things considered but as I followed him through the door I had second thoughts about it. His shoulders were almost as wide as the opening and I thought that if I had to bet on the outcome my money would be on him, a win in the fourteenth by a KO.

When the sparring began my revised forecast was confirmed. He was a strong, skilled fighter, fencing and banging away with equal facility. Soon the claret was decanting from my flattened nose. A second blow almost put me to sleep and I only managed to keep my feet by hanging on to him like a limpet. When he managed to push me off I loosed a hopeless roundhouse and it caught him solidly on the side of the head. It was the first punch I'd got home and it slowed him, but not enough. He banged another into my face, splitting my lower lip and I sucked it into my mouth to assess the damage. It was minor, a shallow cut and the weak spot, my upper lip, was still intact. But the spurt of blood encouraged him, not red in the yellow light from the lamps but black like soot. There were smears of it on his face.

He kept peppering my face and drumming my ribs and I couldn't do a lot to stop him. But I kept close, barring him from the leverage that would give speed and power to his punches. That made it safe to leave him, pecking away, punching himself out. He did tire after a while and I tried another haymaker. It went home as easily as the first and sat him down.

It was plain that he could not see punches coming in from the side. At last I had the answer to his greater skill and for the first time in the contest was confident that I would not spend Christmas in hospital after all. When he got up I landed my third blow of the fight and it sat him down again. I kept doing it. Soon I was sick of it. Dover was game with too much courage for his own good. He would keep on getting to his feet and I would have to go on knocking him down. He was beaten but would not admit it, a strength of will that I admired. I understood what he was doing and why, so there was a choice, either pound him to death or offer him my hand. I gave him my hand and he took it without question. It seemed that he knew me as well as I knew him.

Next morning I was told to report to Major Woodhouse. It was 23 December but I didn't think that the summons had anything to do with the presentation of an early Christmas present. He would know about the fight of course; his intelligence service was extensive but that could not be the reason either, or at least I hoped not. In the past fair fights were not matters for investigation, but so many regimental rules had been changed recently that anything was possible. When I entered his office I kept that in mind, ready for any surprises he might spring on me.

As always the Major was sparing with words yet the Christmas spirit seemed to be rising in him. He smiled, noticed my lower lip, looked thoughtful, then smiled again and nodding, a sign that he knew how I had come by it. He reached into a drawer in his desk and brought out a red beret, placing it carefully on the desktop, then took something out of his breast pocket and laid it beside the beret: it was the winged sword insignia of the SAS. He looked at them for some moments and then spoke. 'You have been wearing a khaki beret, why?'

'I gave my red one to a friend.'

'Oh, why was that, who was it?'

'A Royal Marine sir, Pat Gallagher.'

'A marine, where?'

'At Kota Tinggi. He was on the signals course with me.'

'Oh yes, and what did you do with your spare?'

'It was stolen sir.'

'By another friend?' The Old Fox was enjoying himself and I decided to play along with him.

'Possibly sir, there were thefts at the school.'

My fingers were crossed when I said that. Woodhouse murmured something under his breath, picked up the beret and the badge and handed them to me.

'Don't give it away will you? And don't get it stolen.' I thanked him. 'Get the badge sewn on and wear the beret.'

'Yes sir and thank you again and the compliments of the season to you.'

'Yes and a merry Christmas to you.'

Back in the barrack room I put my mark on the beret with an indelible pencil. Six years later it was stolen.

The Christmas spirit brought a more relaxed air to the barracks; unnecessary duties were cut back and there was time to spare, giving me the opportunity to visit the military hospital in Singapore. Ned Murray and others from the Squadron had been patients there for some time and any break in routine was welcomed by them. On my first visit, other than as a patient, I was pleased to find that Murray was well on the road to recovery – he was complaining.

He wanted out and on this particular occasion his main gripe was that no one would give him a discharge date and he wanted to know why. He kept on and on about it until finally, just to shut him up, I had a word with Nurse 'Juno'.

'He will be out in a week if he behaves himself.'

'What if he doesn't?'

'He will stay.' She was very sure about that and I did not inquire any further into the proviso but the thought of Murray misbehaving was intriguing. What had he been up

The author, wearing the cap badge of the SAS, and an unidentified friend.

to during his convalescence, other than moaning? I would have to ask at a time when he was in a better humour.

'Good news Neddy, you're almost as good as new and will be out in a few days.' But the news did not please him and he started complaining again, making such a row that it brought 'Juno' to the scene.

'What are you going on about now? You have been told that you will be out soon. If you carry on I will personally see to it that you never get out.' He believed her and quietened down.

We gossiped, swapping snippets of information for half an hour. Then, right out of the blue he mentioned the round robin and his willingness to sign it. His casual reference to what I'd believed to be a secret known only to members of the committee and those who had actually signed set me back on my heels. How had he found out? I didn't ask. It was enough that he did. Neither of the two canvassers had been near the hospital so the information had not come from them. Clearly the round robin was now an open secret leaked by one of the 21 signatories. But that was no bad thing. Our purpose had been to make our wishes known to the ACO. Now he would know and the whole purpose of the exercise was complete.

The fly in the ointment was the continuing existence of the paper, damning evidence that would be used against us if found. It had to be destroyed. I had to get back to the barracks as quickly as possible, contact the holder and do what was necessary.

When leaving the hospital by a side gate I saw Sergeant Hanna and the SSM sitting in a jeep parked outside the main entrance. My immediate thought was that I was too late to do anything. The paper had been found and I was now about to be arrested. When I came alongside the vehicle they looked up and recognised me but showed no surprise, not even when I asked if they were going back to the barracks. Yes, they were and yes, I could have a lift. I sat on one of the rear seats next to Hanna and the SSM started the engine. The ride to Selarang was silent for the most part but that was not out of the ordinary. Neither of my travelling companions were noted conversationalists. In fact if either of them had spoken more than a greeting it would have gone a long way towards confirming my suspicions concerning their presence outside the hospital. And yet I had not been formally arrested. But then I was in the company of two cunning old soldiers who would always play things the easy way if it was on offer. Perhaps they were waiting to arrive at the guardroom before giving me the glad tidings. My confidence waned a little when considering this.

We reached the barracks and the SSM stopped the jeep near the guardroom. As was usual Pete Kerry was duty provost and he raised the barrier. Surely now the moment for my arrest, and I did not feel as badly about it as I'd thought I would. There was plenty of good company in the guardroom. But nothing happened, and when they dropped me off outside D Squadron's office I wished them Merry Christmas and went on my way.

I now had to track down the holder of the paper and it proved to be easier than I had imagined. After trying the barrack room and the mess hall I got lucky at my third port of call, running him to earth in the wet canteen. He, even sharper than I had thought and acting on the same information, had already destroyed it – the fact that the round robin's existence was known throughout the barracks and the brass meant that its object had been achieved and there was no longer any need to retain the only real evidence against us.

That being so I wondered why Hanna and the SSM had been waiting outside the BMH. Their object, quite obviously, had been to get me back to the barracks. The provosts, more usually entrusted with such matters, had not been used because I had friends amongst them who would have tipped me the wink. But having arrived at the barracks why had I not been arrested? I guessed that it had been assumed the paper would be found before my return, in which case a reception committee would have greeted me at the camp gates. Everything was known without it of course but that was not enough to butter the parsnips, nothing could be proved.

I left the mess hall to search out the other conspirators. They had to know the state of play. There was a faint possibly that one of them would be pulled in for questioning and fooled into an admission believing that the paper still existed. All were contacted by 11.00pm. It had been a long day and all at once I was tired, turning in as soon as I got to the barrack room.

Next morning, Christmas Day, I was up early to attend mass while the rest of my companions slept on. Afterwards I spoke to some of the congregation, a cross-section of the population including surprisingly, two Malays, a race predominately Muslim. They were a pleasant couple and after speaking together for a while they asked if I would share their Christmas meal, but I had to refuse, explaining that Christmas lunch in the British Army was a repast that no soldier would miss. My refusal was taken in good spirits and another offer was made, a lift back to the barracks, which I accepted.

The Regiment was up and about when I got back and in a festive mood, though a few were under the weather, gagging on a hair of the dog they had swallowed whole on the previous night. In the barrack room I exchanged good wishes with everyone. Corporal Dover was back on form and we chatted for a while. He was wearing an eye patch which suited him, giving him a piratical look, a token of the work I had done on his face. The bruises on my ribs were not so heroic and after a Tiger or two they would be forgotten.

As always the Christmas dinner was special, the cooks excelling, the waiters, particularly the Old Fox, doing hero's work. All went well, the only flash point coming when photographs were being taken, some of the men objecting to the inclusion of the designation '22 SAS' in a group photograph. It was not a protest so much as a hankering after the recent past, a denial of the death of the Malayan Scouts. The problem was solved when one of them stretched his arm across the board, the sign then showing that they were Malayan Scouts, nothing added. The rest of the photographs were taken without props.

If the cooks excelled in the preparation of the feast — and the majority agreed that they had — the quartermaster ran them a close second, the beer cool and sufficient to take us into the night. I did as much as anyone to run it out but failed, retreating in darkness to the barrack room. Most of the bunks were occupied and that was pleasing. I had not been the first to call it quits after all.

I lay awake, thinking about the day's events and glad that I wouldn't have to rise so early the next day, sleeping on like my comrades, having no mass to attend. A few years ago they would have had to rise with me, church parades being compulsory for everyone, Muslims, Catholics, Jews, and members of the Church of England were required to attend the service.

One place particularly notorious for the strict observance of the practice was the army depot just outside Elgin in the Scottish highlands, where I was based for a time

resembling a riding crop, business end uppermost. They are firmly in place from the beginning and when pushed aside, spring back like the poles on a ski slalom.

The swamp is home to numerous crabs and mudskipper fish, the latter as happy on or in the mud as they are in the water – and they are very good to eat. On our first night on the coast they were my supper, but not before I caught several crabs, thinking them a better meal. However, on cracking one open and seeing the meagre amount of meat inside the shell I threw it away and released the other captives. Once free I'd expected them to get away as quickly as possible but they didn't, instead making a beeline for the remains of their recently executed relative. On arrival they fell to and devoured him. It was obvious that I was in a waste not, want not society and hardly in a position to judge. After all if the deceased had been a little plumper I'd have eaten him myself, and his relatives as well. It was sunset before I ran down enough mudskippers to make a decent meal. They were too small to gut so I cooked them as they were – heads and tails and other things taste as well as rump steak if eaten in the dark.

Patrolling the salt swamp was as easy as walking a ridge. The mud was shallow with the consistency of crisp snow. I wonder what would be said if I asked for a pair of snowshoes to expedite my progress through it? Six months previously I'd probably have got them but times had changed and any such request would now be treated as an attempt to ridicule my betters.

Lying in ambush at the edge of the forest looking out into the mangroves was a much more rewarding task than doing the same on a narrow jungle track. There was a vista to the sea and beyond that the sky seemed limitless, giving a feeling of total freedom. Once settled beneath the trees we became part of the landscape. Nothing disturbed us. Leeches and mosquitoes stayed away, repelled by the salt in the mud and air.

The tiger came in the late afternoon. I was on the left flank of the position and heard the noise of its movements clearly. It was to the left, within the forest, moving slowly towards the swamp. It stilled the usual sounds, the swish of movement clear as a bell. I eased the safety catch on my rifle and waited for a body to appear, not knowing then what the creature was. It would be alright to kill the man but wrong to kill a deer, giving our position away to no purpose. So I was patient, waiting to view before killing. Then it appeared.

It was close, about five yards away, near enough to hear the purr in its throat and to see its teeth, long and finely pointed, a male about six years old. It moved out of the forest and paused before the swamp, moving its head from side to side like the pendulum of a clock. Then it turned and looked to where we were, its yellow eyes unblinking. It could not see us but knew we were there and was not concerned. When curiosity was satisfied it turned and looked into the swamp again. We had been given enough attention and now it walked out into the mud, yawned and lay down. It was taking a mud bath. It stayed for almost an hour. Then it left in the way it had come and disappeared into the forest. I listened to the rustle of movement until it faded. Soon afterwards the monkeys began to chatter again. They had been aware of it longer than I and were now letting everyone know that it had gone.

The author (second from right) with a Scout patrol group.

Operation *Titus* continued. Forest and swamp were quartered, searched from end to end. The killers of Carney were not there. They had remained, as I knew they would have, in the area they had occupied since 1948. More than seven years after our hopeless search the leader of the group, Ah Hoi, who had led his regiment against the Japanese in Selangor almost as well as Lao Lee had in Pahang, was offered terms, accepted and came out of the forest. He and the remnants of his command were handsomely rewarded by the government, absolved after ten years from effective control of the state. If a tenth of the per capita sum handed out then had been given in 1945 to those who had fought England's enemies so well, the war that erupted in 1948 would not have happened. By then the communist guerrillas and guerrillas who were not communists would have been small-holders, able to support their families without the need to go cap in hand to ask for employment from those who might or might not have been on very friendly terms with the Japanese.

Lao Lee died in the forest under a hail of bullets. He was killed by men from a country he had always admired, loving what he saw as the 'English way'. In 1945 he had wanted to become a part of that more than anything else in the world. But it was not to be. Instead he was forced into the place that he was never to leave.

Titus ended without a massive use of helicopters. There were no evacuations, no men lost through fever or exhaustion. Everyone that went in came out again. It was the last hurrah of the Malayan Scouts, for that was what we were, if not on paper.

20

THE END OF THE WAR

When the Regiment was withdrawn from operational duties at the end of 1951 there was persistent talk of parachuting as a quick response tactic. In the ranks opinion was divided as to its value but the officers were in favour – it would shorten the war they said. No thought was given to the consequences of parachuting men into a heavily wooded area, a sure way to break bones. There was also the question of security. Secrecy of movement is the essence of success in jungle warfare and quick response is of no value if the enemy is aware of it. And they would be, tipped off by the noise from the transport planes, alerting every guerrilla along the flight path and in the operational area, giving them ample time to plan their response. If in strength they could stand and fight with an excellent chance of winning. Paras are vulnerable, in the air, when they land, and until clear of the chute harness. Once in the trees they would be sitting ducks for those awaiting them below, coming under fire without the means of returning it. If the guerrillas chose to run they would be out of reach before the first parachute snagged in the canopy, making the whole effort an expensive waste of time and equipment. After discussion the ORs dismissed the ideas as the most harebrained scheme ever dreamed up. A few dissented, the SAS had used parachutes in the past so why not in the present? Because parachuting into open spaces in Europe was a different matter. It seemed that the glamour attached to airborne operations in the Second World War was blurring the vision of those who were paid to think clearly. In spite of the arguments against, those in favour won the day and the era of the parachute came once again to the SAS.

The first operational drop took place in the Belum valley close to the Siamese border in February 1952. It was a qualified success, no deaths or serious injuries occurring, everyone getting to the ground eventually. Some had been stranded in the trees for a time, the ropes issued to enable them to reach the jungle floor too short for the purpose. Fortunately there had been no reception committee awaiting them. At the end of the operation the net gain was the knowledge that the trees in Malaya were

A helicopter evacuates yet another Malayan Scout.

higher than had been allowed for. The fact that there was no guerrilla activity either
during or after the drop, while not proof positive that the insurgents had moved out
on the approach of the aircraft, was sufficient to show the limitations of parachutists in
an operational role. It was enough to confirm the argument against but was ignored
and the game went on.

In 1954 three men were killed when the branches on which their chutes had
snagged broke, plunging them to the ground 250 feet below. Others were injured and
had to be evacuated by helicopter. Before that could take place a landing strip had to
be prepared, involving many hours of backbreaking work. It was now plain to all that
the quick response theory did not work in practice and it was put aside. But instead
of abandoning the parachute, a new scheme was found in which it could be used. The
insurgents grew food crops in clearings deep in the forest, ideal targets and excellent
drop zones. The destruction of the crops now became the reason for the continuance
of the policy. Again the reasoning was flawed. The food growing areas were known
because of aerial surveillance and their destruction could be brought about very easily
using the planes that had been the means of their discovery. The RAF had been dropping bombs into the jungle for six years, the only result being the deaths of one or two
monkeys. Now it had properly defined targets that could be razed at a quarter of the
cost of a parachute operation. Strangely it was not considered for the role. Cost and
effectiveness it seemed were not to be taken into account.

While the special aptitudes of the RAF were ignored in one way they were made
use of in another. Bombers flattened areas of the forest to make safe DZs, the irony of
the act going over the heads of the originators of the tree jumping policy. The DZs

not dependable enough to be trusted with intelligence matters. That had been ably demonstrated when the police had taken control of what should have been left to them. It seemed that they were not to be trusted even with purely military matters.

One thing of benefit to the Regiment resulted from the operation. Tree jumping was finally put aside. The Telok Anson adventure had proved once again that it was a hindrance, causing casualties, wasting time, losing the element of surprise and gain-ing nothing. Some years later, the Old Fox, by then CO of the Regiment, made this clear to all concerned and clear also to those endeavouring to make it their concern. The Regiment was no longer a toy, the men no longer chess pieces. It did not exist to amuse grown-up children. The resurrection of the old was not welcomed other than within the Regiment but the Fox stuck to his guns and prevailed. There are few junior field officers who will cross swords with the top brass and come out best in the contest. Woodhouse did because of his time with the free spirits of the Malayan Scouts in the early, hard days of the Regiment. They showed him that men remained men in spite of any particular circumstance and that one was as good as another until proved otherwise. He had not made the Scouts, they had made him and whatever else he became they would always see him as one of their own.

It is said that Woodhouse was the father of 22 SAS, or was it Calvert? In fact the true fathers of the Regiment were the men of the Malayan Scouts. They were together for a year, the strongest, most colourful characters in the army, frightening friends and enemies alike, even their own officers. More than 50 years later the mere mention of their names is an excuse to put everything else aside and tell tales and boast. When old soldiers meet they speak of them, pricking their ears when a name is mentioned, glee-fully boasting that they knew him, had soldiered alongside him.

Soon after the end of the war the people of Singapore, using the votes gained for them by men like myself and my friends, elected a leader who had presented himself as a populist. But within a very short space of time he assumed dictatorial power, fill-ing the jails and keeping the hangman busy for many years. Malaya remained at the disposal of a multitude of sultans and sultanas, each with the authority of a Sun King. The British soldier left, having made the country safe for those who ruled to indulge themselves. They had other wars to fight that were not wars. It was what they were paid to do. They had six shillings a day for doing it.

EPILOGUE

It is said that during the short life of the Malayan Scouts that there was constant turmoil in the Regiment. In fact the turmoil only began when that life was coming to an end. The men wanted the Regiment to remain as it was and when they saw changes being made they did what they could to stop them. They were not concerned about the change of name. It was their belief that they had been Malayan Scouts and members of the SAS from the very beginning and had no objections to losing one of their titles, being known solely as the 22nd SAS Regiment. A spade remains a spade whatever it is called. Their concerns were about the fundamental changes to the Regiment's ethos: the loss of consultation between officers and men and that of absolute trust between all ranks fostered by Colonel Calvert. Such matters, added to a change in the perceived view and function of discipline was seen as the end of the commonwealth of the Regiment. Not that the men were foolish to the point where they believed that self regulated discipline would be equally beneficial in a line regiment, they knew it would not. They did believe that a special force needed a special type of management if it was to function effectively. This was not in evidence after December 1951 when they saw themselves coming under the control of officers with no experience of special forces and obviously no understanding of the motivations that made such forces work.

The free and easy ways of the Scouts was a bone of contention. They were not always respectful to their superiors, sometimes they saluted and other times they didn't. And when they had money they spent it on drink and sometimes had enough to get drunk. Childish tricks were played on those who wanted

253 **A MODERN CAMPAIGN SERVICE PAIR: Private J.C. Durkin, Malayan Scouts (S.A.S.):** War Medal, 1939-45 (*unnamed as issued*), General Service Medal, 1918, George VI, 1 clasp, Malaya (Pte., Malayan Scouts (S.A.S.)), this last an official re-impressed replacement issue, *mounted for wearing, very fine or better* (2)   £140–160
Sold with a series of correspondence regarding the recipient's claim to have his replacement G.S.M. named in the above manner, his being the only G.S.M. so inscribed. He saw service in Malaya under Mike Calvert, C.O. of the Malayan Scouts, which subsequently became 22nd S.A.S.

Sergeant E. Lillico, ready for battle.

to be taken seriously. They indulged in, and encouraged fist fighting and duelling. However, the fact remained that the Scouts were the most effective counter-guerrilla force in Malaya. They may well have frightened some of the newer officers, who decided that officers had to be shown respect, whatever their worth.

Towards the end of 1951 when the new order was already partly in place, scant if any attention was paid to the possibility that it could harm the cohesion of the Regiment. A new way of going about things did not necessarily mean a better way, particularly so when introduced to replace one that had worked in the past. Calvert's mantra was self discipline, to know when to disobey, remaining committed to the object of the soldier, to win. That principle was imbued in the Scouts who accepted and practised it, becoming captains of their own souls. The new way, instinct cowed to discipline, was shown to be flawed many times in the following years, such as in Borneo in early 1965. A patrol led by a Sergeant Lillico came under fire, and he and the leading scout, Trooper Thompson, were hit, suffering serious wounds. In spite of their injuries both men returned fire pinning their attackers down. During a lull in the exchange Sergeant Lillico, separated from Thompson and unable to see his injuries, shouted to him to fall back and bring up the rest of the patrol. Unknown to Lillico, Thompson was crippled but carried out the instruction crawling on his stomach, pulling himself along using his arms as levers. On hearing the initial small arms fire the main body of the patrol, some way behind, took up defensive positions at the side of the track. They remained there as the skirmish continued and after about ten minutes fell back to summon reinforcements. In doing so they were obeying the standing order for dealing with such situations though the circumstances merited ignoring it. Initiative had been drilled out of them. By the time Thompson arrived with the order to advance it was too late – they had gone, victims of a philosophy that left no room for manoeuvre.

By March 1952, A Squadron – the most senior in the Regiment – was decimated, not by the enemy but from within. The free spirits of B and D Squadrons were also exorcised, disappearing from the Regiment day by day. All those considered too hard to handle were struck from the roll. A few men remained, enough to ensure the survival of the Regiment and the concept that brought it into being. In time it would return to first principles. But before that there was to be a long period in which the discipline of the barrack square was judged more important than the real purpose of the Regiment. When that period passed there was a return to the beginning, vindicating Calvert, the Scouts, his way and their way. His words to the men of D Squadron in June 1951 had proved prophetic. 'Persist and you will win.' The Scouts who remained in the Regiment after March 1952 did persist, ensuring that the ethos of the Malayan Scouts became part of the SAS.

GLOSSARY

Ac dum	carry out quickly
ACO	Acting Commanding Officer
Atap	native thatched huts made of the leaves of the Nipa palm
Basha	An improvised shelter usually made from waterproof canvas or a trooper's poncho
Belukar	cleared land that has reverted to jungle
BMH	British Military Hospital
BORs	British Other Ranks
Charpoy	light Indian bedstead
Commons	rations
DSO	Distinguished Service Order
DZ	drop zone
GOC	General Officer Commanding
Godown	a warehouse, especially one at a dockside
HE	high explosive
JG	Jungle Greens
Kampong	village
KARs	King's African Rifles
Kati	a unit of weight
KIA	killed in action
KRR	King's Rules and Regulations
MO	Medical Officer
Naik	military rank of Corporal in the former British Indian Army
OC	Officer Commanding
OIC	Officer in Command
OO	Orderly Officer
ORs	Other Ranks

Panga	A large cleaver-like cutting tool
Panee	to drink
Percheron	a strong and swift horse bred in le Perle, a district of France
Poilu	a friendly term for a French First World War infantryman
PE	plastic explosive
QMS	Quarter Master Sergeant
RAAF	Royal Australian Air Force
RAP	Regimental Aid Post
RASC	Royal Army Service Corps
RFC	Royal Flying Corps
RHQ	Regimental Headquarters
RP	Regimental Police
RPS	Regimental Provost Sergeant
RSM	Regimental Sergeant Major
R/T	radio transmitter
RV	rendezvous
Sakia	An indigenous people of the Malay Peninsula used as trackers, porters and guides by the Malayan Scouts
SMO	Senior Medical Officer
SSM	Squadron Sergeant Major
Tuans	used in Malay as a respectful address for a man, equivalent to sir or mister
Ulu	the jungle or 'out there'

INDEX